# THE ESSEX HUNDRED HISTORIES

## 100 EVENTS AND PERSONALITIES THAT SHAPED THE NATION'S HISTORY

### With National and International Timelines

*Andrew Summers
and John Debenham*

*Illustrated by
Elizabeth Summers*

www.essex100.com

Published by Summersbook (UK) Ltd
Rutland House
90 – 92 Baxter Avenue
Southend-on-Sea
Essex SS2 6HZ

www.essex100.com

First published June 2008
Reprinted September 2008
Reprinted November 2008
Reprinted May 2009
Written by Andrew Summers and John Debenham
Illustrated by Elizabeth Summers
© Copyright Andrew Summers
and John Debenham 2008
All rights reserved.

British library cataloguing in Publication Data -
A catalogue record for this book is available from
The British Library.

ISBN 0955229510
9780955229510

Typeset and printed by 4edge Publishing
7a Eldon Way
Eldon Way Industrial Estate
Hockley Essex SS5 4AD

# CONTENTS

**The King of Bling**

# INTRODUCTION

From the Romans - to nuclear power and the Space Shuttle. How and why has Essex played such a pivotal role in the development of British History? Some interesting facts and unusual events make up the remarkable history of Essex.

Daniel Defoe, the great English novelist, wrote in his book, *A Tour through the whole Island of Great Britain,*

"I set out, the 3rd of April 1722, passing Bow-Bridge where the county of Essex begins."

Essex is one of our oldest counties and derived its name from the sixth century Kingdom of the East Saxons. It is naturally bounded by rivers: Thames to the south, Lea to the west, Stour to the north and to the east by the North Sea, (formerly called the German Ocean). It has remained unchanged since its emergence as a county, or autonomous region, until local government reorganisation in 1965. This meant the loss of the south-western corner of the county to create the London Boroughs of Waltham Forest, Redbridge, Newham, Barking and Havering. Nevertheless for the purpose of this book 'Essex' is taken to mean the 'Natural County' of pre-1965 and as far back as Roman times.

The 'Hundred' was the ancient system of land measurement dating from Saxon times. It was a subdivision of a county or shire and had its own court. It consisted of 100 hides, or parcels of land, each capable of supporting a family, which could be an extended family of up to fifty people. In 1085 William the Conqueror sent Royal Commissioners across the country to assess land and property holdings in order to settle continuous disputes over the collection of taxes. The result was the 'Domesday Book', a definitive account, which gave the county of Essex seventeen 'Hundreds' plus for good measure some 'Half Hundreds' too! (See map page 100).

The one hundred topics we have taken from the history of Essex, as with most histories, revolve around people of strong character: The good, bad, eccentric and the just plain unlucky. Many have had profound effects on wider national, and sometimes international, histories.

The 'good' would include the Leigh Fishermen who so unselfishly sailed their *'Little Ships of Leigh'* to Dunkirk, and *'The Lady on the Five Pound Note'*, Elizabeth Fry, who from her home in East Ham worked tirelessly for prison reform.

The 'bad' were such as Hempstead's ruthlessly evil Dick Turpin whose cry of, *'Stand and Deliver!'*, was heard all over the county. Also Lord Richard Rich who during the *'Dissolution'* acquired Leez Priory and, in 2005 in a BBC History Magazine poll, was nominated the worst Briton of the 16th century. He was also voted the third worst of the last 1,000 years and yet is remembered in Felsted for his generosity!

For 'eccentricity' we may look to Dunmow's Lionel Lukin who on inventing the unsinkable lifeboat tested it in the village *'Doctor's Pond'*. As for the 'plain unlucky' was there a woman of strong character ever more unlucky than Rochford's Ann Boleyn? Although able *'To Marry a King'*, she lost her head just through being unable to produce a son!

Our first book **The Essex Hundred** illustrated these events through the medium of poetry. Our aim in this book has been to dig a little deeper into the same one hundred topics and some of the ancillary or secondary characters. These topics cover a period of two thousand years, from the battles of *'Boudica'* in AD 60 to today's electricity generating *'Windmills'* adorning the Dagenham skyline.

For convenience we have separated the book into four time periods. For each of these we have included a 'Timeline' to give a global background to what was happening in Essex.

In order to provide factual and, as far as possible, historical accuracy, our research has led us to the four corners of the county, including some areas we were previously quite unfamiliar with.

On the banks of the Thames at Tilbury we looked over the site where Elizabeth I, in 1588, rallied her troops with the words *'I know I have the body of a weak and feeble woman'*. Then on the county's northern border the tiny village of Gestingthorpe was the home of Captain Oates who sacrificed his life saying *'I may be some time'* on Scott's ill fated Antarctic expedition. From the Lea Valley of *'William Morris'* childhood in the west we travelled to the ancient village of Pagelsham, the 18th century 'Smuggling Capital of the East Coast' and home of William *'Hard Apple'* Blyth, local hero and notorious smuggler.

Criss-crossing the county our investigations have been interesting, enlightening but above all enjoyable. The list of places and contact addresses at the end of the book is included in order to help any reader wishing to explore further. To those that do so we wish well and hope you gain as much pleasure from your efforts as we have had in researching for the book.

## ACKNOWLEDGEMENTS

Feedback from many readers of **The Essex Hundred** suggested that, while enjoying the poetry, they would have liked more factual background than the short notes we were able to provide. The result is this book and we thank all those readers for their useful and encouraging comments.

In bringing **The Essex Hundred Histories** to publication, research has taken us to all parts of the county. We have received help and encouragement from churchwardens, curators, archivists, editors, librarians, the press office of Ford Motor Company and many others. Without them the book would not have been possible and we are indebted to them. In particular we thank Shirley Baker for her reading and invaluable editorial suggestions, Adele Fewings for her work on the **Essex Hundred** website and Joanna Debenham for her diligent proof reading. Special thanks are due to our wives, Greg Debenham and Glenis Summers, who have provided support throughout, and made some incisive observations when they were most needed.

The extracts of poems heading each history are from our previous book and are used with the permission of the authors for which we are grateful.

The valuable work that many local historians undertake is often copied and quoted in other media without credit or reference back to the source material. We have tried to make our bibliography (Page 199) as comprehensive as possible and have acknowledged quotations or direct contributions in the text. In-depth historical research requires the skills of a forensic detective in following leads and the patience of a saint to spend many hours in record offices or libraries whether studying archive material or simply collections of memorabilia such as old postcards. As far as Essex is concerned we acknowledge our debt to a few of those whose work we have been fortunate to be able to draw on. Our list, in alphabetical order, is certainly not exhaustive - Randal Bingley (Thurrock), Douglas Carter (Boxted), Robert Hallman (Benfleet), Silvia Kent (Billericay), Norman Jacobs (Clacton), Reg Bush (Sandon) and Ian Yearsley (Southend). Apologies to any we have missed.

*Andrew Summers*
*John Debenham*

# TIMELINE

| ESSEX EVENT COMMEMORATED | DATE AD | NATIONAL OR INTERNATIONAL EVENT |
|---|---|---|
| | 43 | *Romans Invade England* |
| Boudica (Boadicea) sacks Colchester | 60 | *London designated capital of Britain* |
| Kingdom of the East Saxons founded | 500 | *St. David, Patron Saint of Wales born* |
| King Saebert buried in Prittlewell | 630 | *Mohammad captures Mecca* |
| St Cedd founds community at Othona | 654 | *Benedictines come to Peterborough* |
| Battle of Benfleet | 893 | *Bishop Asser writes ' Life of King Alfred'* |
| Harold interred at Waltham Abbey | 1066 | *Battle of Hastings* |
| Sweyn's Castle built at Rayleigh | 1070 | *Hereward the Wake - Saxon Revolt* |
| Guernons become Monfichet | 1071 | *Norman invasion of Ireland* |
| Robert de Vere oversees Magna Carta | 1215 | *Magna Carta signed at Runnymede* |
| Castle Hedingham falls to King John | 1216 | *King John succeeded by Henry III* |
| Hadleigh Castle started | 1219 | *Newgate Prison founded in London* |
| Edward III stays in Boxted | 1354 | *Birth of Owen Glendower* |
| Peasants revolt begins in Brentwood | 1381 | *Peasants revolt ends at Smithfield* |
| Death of John Hawkwood | 1394 | *Richard II goes to Ireland* |
| Duke of Gloucester seized at Pleshey | 1396 | *Gloucester murdered in Calais* |
| First recorded Pie Powder Court in Essex | 1398 | *Teutonic Order occupies Gotland* |
| Richard Wright claims 'Dunmow Flitch' | 1445 | *Birth of Sandro Botticelli* |
| Edmund Tudor leaves Barking Abbey | 1441 | *Eton College founded* |
| Henry Marney supports Henry Tudor for English Crown | 1485 | *Richard III dies at Bosworth Field Henry VII is first of Tudor dynasty* |
| Construction of Layer Marney Tower | 1500 | *First Caesarean birth in Switzerland* |
| Death of Lord Marney | 1523 | *Birth of Martín Cortés, conquistador* |
| Thomas Poyntz smuggles bibles | 1536 | *Willian Tyndale burnt at the stake* |
| Ann Boyleyn beheaded | 1536 | *Michaelangelo paints Sistine Chapel* |
| Leez Priory acquired by Lord Rich | 1537 | *Dissolution of Monasteries continues* |
| Hadleigh Castle sold to Lord Rich | 1552 | *St Andrews Golf Club founded* |
| Richard Asser convicted at Maldon | 1556 | *Tobacco introduced to England* |
| 'Baron' Rich founds Felsted School | 1564 | *Birth of William Shakespeare* |
| Harbingers inspect Mark Hall in Harlow | 1576 | *Martin Frobisher explores Canada* |
| Walden becomes Saffron Walden | 1582 | *William Shakespeare marries Anne Hathaway* |
| Queen Elizabeth I speaks in Tilbury | 1588 | *Spanish Armada defeated* |
| William Byrd moves to Stondon Massey | 1589 | *William Shakespeare writes - 'The Two Gentlemen of Verona'* |

**Boudica's monument on the river Thames opposite
the House of Parliament in Westminster**

# BOADICEA'S REVENGE ON CAMULODUNUM

*Brandishing her arms*
*The Lioness roared*

Boadicea, or Boudicca, is one of Britain's greatest heroines. She is remembered for her challenge to the dominance of the Romans after they had broken their agreement with her husband and humiliated her. When Prasutagus, King of the Iceni kingdom of East Anglia, died in AD 60, his will promised control of half of his realm to the Romans, and half to his wife, Queen Boudicca. The Romans reneged on the agreement after his death. They sacked the Iceni capital of Thetford and Queen Boudicca was publicly whipped and her two daughters raped.

Boudicca, a proud Queen, determined to avenge her people and her family. Joining forces with the Trinovantes, an Essex tribe, she mustered an army of almost 100,000 strong. With this enthusiastic but undisciplined force she chose to exact revenge on the important Roman City of Camulodunum; modern day Colchester.

Colchester Castle Museum stands on the foundations of the Roman 'Temple of Claudius' which, according to the Roman historian Tacitus, "The local population regarded as a citadel of tyranny". The Romans, vastly outnumbered by the rebels, took refuge in the temple but to no avail. They were overwhelmed, put to the sword and the city burnt to the ground. Evidence of the burning survives to this day in what is known as 'Boudicca's Destruction Horizon.' It is said that digging almost anywhere in Colchester will come to a thick layer of red soot. There is in fact a glass panel in the cellar of the George Hotel in the High Street through which can be seen the distinctive burnt red clay.

Boudicca's triumph at Colchester led to the swelling of her army to over 200,000. She marched on, destroying Londinium and then Verulamium, modern St Albans. She had succeeded but her victory was short lived.

On his return from campaigning in Wales, the Roman Governor Suetonius Paulinus organised a strong and disciplined army, which defeated the Britons decisively in a battle somewhere north of St Albans where, to avoid capture, Boudicca is believed to have killed herself.

Lewis Spence, in his book 'Boadicea Warrior Queen of the Britons,' suggested that the final battle took place on the site of Kings Cross train station. This led to a popular myth that Boudicca was in fact buried under platform 9. We will probably never know where she lies. Archaeologists have posed sites for the last battle as far apart as Staffordshire and Surrey but all would agree that our heroine's fame began with Colchester.

# KING OF BLING??

*In a simple wooden coffin he was laid to rest*
*His eyes with two golden crosses were blest*

In 2004, close to Priory Park in Southend, archaeologists, in advance of a proposed road widening scheme, made a surprise discovery - a complete and undefiled Saxon burial chamber dating from the early $7^{th}$ century.

The only reliable history of this period is the *'Ecclesiastical History of the English Peoples'* completed by the benedictine monk, The Venerable Bede, in AD 731. In it he wrote of a King Saebert reigning over the East Saxons in A.D. 604. Saebert died in 616 and it is possible that it was his burial chamber that was discovered. Examination of its contents has led to much supposition in support of this.

King Saebert, or Saebba as some call him, came to Christianity through his uncle Aethelbert King of Kent. When he died it would seem that he desired to be buried as his faith required and was laid to rest in a simple wooden coffin, the only reference to his religion being two gold foil crosses that could have been laid on his eyes.

His sons however would appear to have had different ideas. Tired of being dominated by Christian Kent they rebelled against their father's faith and turned to traditional pagan practice. It would be another generation on before Christianity came back. St Cedd arrived at Bradwell to convert Saebert's grandson, King Sigeberht in 654, and built the Cathedral Church of St Peter's.

To our good fortune the ideas of Saeward, Seaxred and Seaxbald, the King's sons prevailed. Their father was buried as befitted someone of his noble birth, wealth and status. Saebert was given everything he might need for his journey in the next life. The chamber was bedecked with, among other things, drinking vessels, cooking and eating utensils, valued personal possessions and weapons. Some of these items would have been hanging from iron hooks riveted to the walls but many were carefully arranged around the body. Music was not forgotten since remains were found of an instrument resembling a lyre.

The burial chamber has proved a treasure trove throwing much light on early Saxon Essex. It has been said that it is the most important find since the graves at Sutton Hoo in Suffolk were excavated in the nineteen-eighties. Of the quality of the artefacts and the wealth and status of the occupant of this grave there can be no doubt. That it was indeed King Saebert must for the time being at least remain supposition since no actual body remained. It would seem though that to call whoever it was 'Southend's King of Bling' may not be wholly inappropriate.

# THE CHAPEL OF ST PETER-ON-THE-WALL

*From ruined Othona grew St Peter's-on-the-Wall*
*And St. Cedd its new Bishop, ministering to all.*

In 654 St Cedd landed on the Essex coast at Bradwell-on-Sea, then called *Ythancaestir*. Invited by King Sigeberht to bring Christianity to his people Cedd built a simple wooden church near the ruins of the old Roman fort of Othona. In time, as his mission grew, he replaced this with the more solid Cathedral Church of St Peter using stone from the Roman ruins. The Chapel of St Peter-on-the-Wall is all that remains today but then the monastic community would have included a school, library, hospital and a guest house. From this base Cedd, as Bishop of the East Saxons, established Christian missions throughout Essex at Mersea, Tilbury, Prittlewell and Upminster. Upon his death from a plague in about 664 St Peter's was taken into the diocese of London, St Paul's, and became a Minster for the surrounding country.

After the Norman invasion, and maybe as a consequence of it, in 1068 St Peter's became the property of the Benedictine Monastery of St Valerie-sur-Somme. It remained under French Benedictine control until 1391 when the estate was bought by Bishop William of Wykeham and brought into English jurisdiction.

As a religious community it flourished until its rapid decline in the seventeen hundreds. For many years after 1750 the Chapel was used as a barn for storing grain and as a shelter for cattle. It was not to be used for religious purposes again until its restoration and re-consecration in 1920.

St Peter's Chapel is now once again part of the community life of Bradwell village. Regular services are held during the summer months. The Chapel is open year round during daylight hours providing visitors with a haven of quiet and shelter from the elements on this often bleak North Sea coast.

A short walk southward along the sea wall from St Peter's is 'The Othona Community.' It was founded by the Revd. Norman Motley, a former RAF chaplain, who wrote, after seeing St Peter's for the first time in 1946, "…the sense of thirteen centuries of prayer was almost overpowering…the moment I entered the building I knew we were home…." He went on to establish a religious community. Taking its name from the old Roman fort the community, with its 'open to all' philosophy, continues to this day

It could be said that St Cedd's surviving monument is St Peter's Chapel. It could also be said that his spirit lives on in the Othona community.

ST PETER-ON-THE-WALL

# The Battle of Benfleet

*Beamfloete: Safe haven for Haesten the Black?*
*The Battle of Benfleet was to change all that.*

In 892 the Danes had planned a large-scale attack on the England of Alfred the Great. The main fleet of 250 ships of their 'Great Army' landed on the south coast of Kent and set up base near Ashford. At the same time Haesten 'The Black' arrived in the Thames estuary with 80 ships. First settling in the village of Milton near Sheppey, Haesten was forced by Alfred to move across the Thames to the Danelaw settlement of Beamfleote, which is now South Benfleet. A Danish community had been established there for some years, working as shipwrights. It was a perfect place from which to launch raids around the coast, into Kent and even up to London. It had fresh water from two streams and was surrounded by forest – the name Beamfleote meant wood and water. Hidden from the estuary's main stream, yet with easy access to the sea, tidal marshes prevented surprise attack from the water.

Having strengthened the existing fortification, Haesten left his wife and children with a garrison guard while he pursued raiding activities further afield. While he was away remnants of the Great Army, defeated by Alfred and chased by his son Edward, had escaped across the Thames and made their way to Benfleet to swell the garrison.

These developments sounded alarm bells to Alfred who was still fighting the invaders in Wessex. Edward, together with Alfred's son-in-law Ethelflaed, raised a fresh army in London. Avoiding what few roads there were, keeping to marsh and forest they marched east along the Thames. They marshalled their forces on the high ground of Hadleigh then swooped on the unsuspecting Danes at Benfleet, storming the fort. Haesten's men were routed, those that survived fled overland to the Danelaw settlement at Shoebury.

With their Fort vanquished all the Viking ships were either destroyed by burning or taken up the river to London. Haesten's wife and two children were captured and also taken to London. Later Alfred ordered their return to Haesten who, in exchange, vowed that he would never again attack England.

In terms of numbers engaged it was not a major battle. It was however decisive and marked the beginning of the end for the Danes. Six years later Alfred died but his descendants were to oversee more than fifty years of peace.

Archaeological surveys have pinpointed the probable site of the anchorage of the Viking ships, which would all have been river and flood marsh. It runs from the Canvey side of the Railway Bridge, through to the drainage streams of 'Church Creek' behind St Mary's Church and comes up behind the Anchor Pub to the back of 'The Moorings' Hall. It is the area from the railway bridge to the Shellfish Stall that is a likely site for the burning of the ships. As to Haesten's Fort, it is thought likely to have been built within the confines of the car park near Benfleet station, between School Lane and the High Street.

A stone memorial to *The Battle of Benfleet,* by sculptor Anthony Lysycia, now stands in the conservation area between Ferry Road and Benfleet Creek.

# NOT A LOT OF PEOPLE KNOW THAT!

*Beside the present church building,*
*An inscription, on a stone lying flat,*
*Reads: 'HAROLD KING OF ENGLAND 1066'*
*Now - 'Not a lot of people know that!'*

The earliest recorded history of Waltham Abbey goes back to King Canute. Towards the end of Canute's reign, in 1034, a blacksmith in the village of Montacute in Somerset discovered a large black flint cross. The cross was removed from the hill and placed in a wagon on the orders of Tovi, the Lord of Montacute, who was also a close advisor to the King. However the beasts (twelve red oxen and twelve white cows) pulling the wagon refused to move. There was much discussion as to what to do and Tovi addressed the crowd gathered around calling for suggestions. Someone shouted, 'Take it to Canterbury', another called 'Winchester' but the cart stood rooted to the ground. Tovi then remarked out loud he was going back to Waltham, where he owned a hunting lodge on the banks of the River Lea, and all of a sudden the cart started to move and appeared to push the animals forward. The wagon, accompanied on its journey by a great throng of people from Montacute, continued non-stop until it reached Essex. Tovi saw it as a sign and decided to build a place of worship on the spot – now Waltham Abbey.

To honour the cross Tovi selected fine jewels to decorate it. However on attempting to fix them with nails to the right arm of the cross it was said that blood suddenly gushed out. Tovi was stunned by this happening. The jewels were immediately removed and placed in a small bag close by and the blood was kept in a silver goblet. So legend grew that just by touching the cross a miracle might happen and Waltham and its cross became a centre of pilgrimage and celebration.

In 1060 Harold Godwinson, Earl of Wessex and later to be the last Saxon King of England, consecrated a new, larger church on the site after apparently being cured of a paralysis there. Harold became King in January 1066 following the death of Edward the Confessor. Edward was alleged to have said to Harold on his deathbed, *I commend my wife and all my kingdom to your care.* Duke William of Normandy however disputed the succession. He asserted that Edward had told him virtually the same thing.

Although supported by most of the English nobility, King Harold soon had other problems to worry about. In September 1066 he had to fight off a large Viking force from Norway who claimed the throne on behalf of their leader, Earl Tostig, who incidentally was Harold's brother.

The Vikings were successfully repelled at the battle of Stamford Bridge but then a more potent threat materialised in Sussex. The Normans had landed in Sussex. Harold hurried south only stopping at Waltham to prostrate himself before the cross. Whilst he lay there on the ground the figure on the cross is said to have looked away. This was seen as an ill-omen, however the King was not told. In view of this the Abbey insisted on sending two of their most trusted brethren, Osegod and Ailric, to accompany Harold to Hastings.

William, Duke of Normandy, having landed with his army had claimed the English throne. In the battle that followed Harold was despatched by that famous arrow in the eye.

Osegod and Ailric saw the King struck down. When the battle was over they began a painstakingly search to find the body. This was very difficult as many of the dead had been stripped and mutilated. Harold's mistress Edith was summoned to Hastings to assist with identification. She recognised certain marks on one of the bodies as belonging to Harold. Immediately the monks asked the victorious William if they could remove the body to Waltham Abbey for burial. Initially William refused but eventually relented. Harold's remains were then collected and carried back to Waltham Abbey. Here Harold was buried with great honour and to this day a memorial stone marks his grave in the Abbey Gardens.

Waltham Abbey became rich from the pilgrims flocking to the *Shrine of the Holy Rood*. It remained wealthy until the time of Henry VIII. In 1540 the Abbey was dissolved and many of the buildings demolished as part of the Kings break with Rome.

As for the stone cross, it disappeared and has never been seen since.

# SWEYN'S CASTLE

*Your castle, Sweyn, is one of imagination*
*A monument to a nation's invaders*
*Almost erased from the town.*

'*Et in hoc manerio fecit Suenue suum castellum*' was the old Latin translated as 'in this manor Sweyn made his castle'. This is written in the Doomsday Book survey of 1086 and Rayleigh is the only castle in Essex that is mentioned.

Although King Harold had been killed and his forces comprehensively defeated by William the Conqueror at the Battle of Hastings there were still elements of Saxon resistance around. Following the victory William dismissed many of the Saxon Lords and confiscated their lands. He then appointed Barons whom he considered loyal and authorised them to build castles at strategic locations around the country. These would serve as fortified strong points that could be defended and reinforced if serious trouble was to break out.

Robert Fitzwimarc was granted the 'Honour' of Rayleigh. Fitzwimarc was a Saxon but was also related to the Normans and some suspected that he gave assistance to the invaders at Hastings.

Rayleigh was in a good position midway between the rivers Crouch and Thames and the Mount afforded commanding views over the local Essex countryside. As an added bonus the estates included woodlands, vineyards, farm animals and the allegiance of all the people living in the area who were tied to the land.

Robert Fitzwimarc died a few years after the Battle of Hastings and it was left to his son Sweyn to construct the Castle. When finished, it was a substantial structure dominating the landscape. Sweyn's son and grandson in turn inherited the Castle and extended and strengthened it. With the land came honours and privileges. Sweyn's grandson Henry de Essex was the King's standard bearer.

King Henry II was actively engaged in suppressing the Welsh. On one of his forays with the King to Wales, Henry de Essex was accused of cowardice in the face of the enemy. Later he was challenged to 'trial by combat', which he lost and was apparently presumed dead. This was not the case as two monks discovered much to their shock when, on retrieving Henry's body, they found he was in fact alive.

Henry De Essex recovered and spent the rest of his life in a monastery in Reading. He never set foot in Rayleigh again. As a consequence of Henry's humiliation the De Essex family was disgraced and the Castle and estate at Rayleigh reverted back to the Kings charge.

The next castle owner by Royal Prerogative was Hubert de Burgh. De Burgh had distinguished himself fighting the French and rose to hold prominent positions during the reign of Henry III. The Rayleigh estate had grown to include the manor of Hadleigh. De Burgh concluded that Hadleigh would be a far superior position for a castle as there were excellent views over the Thames Estuary. With the enemy within vanquished he deemed there was more to fear from the enemy abroad who in any event would come by sea.

The days of Sweyn's Castle as a major fortification were numbered. Richard II would later authorise Rayleigh people to remove its stone for other building work. This may have been a sop to appease the local population who were still seething from the ill-fated peasant's revolt (see pages 32 and 34). Soon the castle was no more and it reverted to farm lands and woods. A visitor today would find little or nothing in the way of fortifications. The Mount is now covered with trees and is a nature reserve administered by the National Trust.

# THE DUKE OF BOULOGNE

*Robert de Guernon fought with William the Conqueror*
*at the battle of Hastings he won victory with honour.*
*a cousin of the King, whose favour he gained,*
*as reward many English estates he obtained.*

Robert de Guernon (or Robert Greno as he is referred to in the Domesday Book), Duke of Boulogne, would seem to have been related to William the Conqueror. He was one of William's commanders in the invasion and decisive victory over King Harold at Hastings in 1066. For his part in the battle William rewarded him with lands and estates in Essex. He became a major landowner in the county. One of his Manors was Ayot Montfitchet and it was here that he made the headquarters of his Barony at the Anglo-Saxon settlement of Stansted. De Guernon built an impressive Norman motte and bailey fortress. The large stone ringwork was surrounded by a wet ditch, or moat, with the bailey having strong ramparts and ditches to the north and east. The castle remained the family seat until the last of the male line, Richard de Montfitchet II, died in 1258. Almost nothing remains today but fragments of twelfth century stonework may be seen on the southern slopes.

On Robert's death his son William inherited the Dukedom and dropped the name of de Guernon, adopting the name 'Montfitchet'. William also founded the Cistercian Abbey at Stratford Longthorne. This was largely destroyed during the dissolution (See page 44). Its remains now lie buried beneath the London Underground Jubilee line, some half a mile south of today's Stratford Broadway.

Of William's son, Gilbert de Montfitchet, little is known. Gilbert's son, Richard, held the office of Forester or Keeper of the Forests of Essex, with the custody of the King's House at Havering and other houses in the Forest, given to him by King Henry II. In 1203, Richard died, leaving his son Richard II a minor. Richard II became a royal ward of King John and was placed in the care of Roger de Lacey, Constable of Chester. As soon as he became of age (the exact date is unknown), Richard de Montfitchet II seems to have joined the Baronial opposition to the monarch incurring the wrath of King John. He joined forces with a group of powerful Essex men that included Robert de Vere of Castle Hedingham, Geoffrey de Mandeville of Pleshey, William de Lanvillei of Colchester, and their leader Robert Fitzwalter Lord of Dunmow. They were some of the twenty-five Barons that rebelled against King John, forcing the signing of the Magna Carta at Runnymede in June 1215.

Before the end of the year John reneged on the promises he had made in the charter, raised an army and set about attacking the Essex rebels.

After successfully laying siege to Castle Hedingham, King John's forces attacked Montfitchet. Though Richard was fortunate and escaped with his life, his stronghold was destroyed. The stone of his ruined castle was subsequently pillaged by local people for house building. The King's victory was short lived; he died the following year at Newark, after famously losing all his treasures crossing the Wash.

Richard de Montfitchet, like many of the rebels, was returned to royal favour by the new King, Henry III, and had all the Montfitchet estates, and what was left of the castle, restored to him. Henry also granted him a Tuesday market at West Ham as well as an annual fair on the 19th to 22nd of July. Both of these were discontinued in the late eighteenth century.

Richard had never married and he died in about 1258. The vast manor of Ayot Montfitchet, or Ayot St Peter as it was also known, was inherited by his three sisters, Margery, Avelina and Phillippa. None of the sisters showed any interest in the castle at Stansted Montfitchet and it remained in ruins. The site became overgrown and lay forgotten for over seven hundred years until its reconstruction in 1984 as a tourist attraction.

Built on the original site the reconstruction accurately depicts the wooden palisaded motte and bailey castle of the eleventh century. Occupying a commanding position overlooking the Stort valley it has throughout history been strategically important. Prior to the Norman invasion and the arrival of Robert de Guernon it had been an Iron Age hill fort, a Roman signals fort and later a Saxon and Viking settlement. For this reason it is a unique time capsule and visitors may step back in history to wander through the Norman village hidden behind the castle walls.

# Magna Carta

*June 15th 1215, at Runnymede King John made his seal*

**The Magna Carta
Seal of 1215**

*The Magna Carta was made law despite last minute appeal.
Robert de Vere, 3rd Earl of Oxford, was appointed to enforce
The Charter with 24 other Barons to ensure it ran its course.*

Robert de Vere was approaching middle age when he inherited Castle Hedingham. On the death of his elder brother Aubrey, in 1214, he became the third Earl of Oxford and Lord Chancellor of England. Aubrey had commanded King John's forces in Ireland, been a Privy Councillor, Steward of Epping Forest and a loyal servant to the monarch.

Robert was to have a quite different relationship with his King. In 1215, together with Richard de Montfitchet, Geoffrey de Mandeville of Pleshey, William de Lanvallei, the Governor of Colchester Castle, and Robert Fitzwalter, Lord of Dunmow he belonged to a group of powerful Essex Barons. They, like many others, were dissatisfied with the running of the country. They threatened to take up arms against the King unless he agreed to reforms which they set out in a charter famously known as the 'Magna Carta'.

The charter that King John signed at Runnymede on 15th June 1215 lies at the root of the British constitution. It was the beginning of all the freedoms that the British people were to gain over the next eight hundred years. It included the clause, *'That laws should be good and fair and that no freeman be imprisoned or punished without going through a proper legal system'.* The document's overriding principle was that the monarch was not above the law. The King could only act in accordance with the legal principles that had been enacted by representatives of the people.

Robert de Vere was one of twenty-five Barons appointed to enforce the King's observance of the charter and their leader was Robert Fitzwalter, Lord of Dunmow. King John claimed that he signed under duress and his subsequent actions demonstrated that he had no intention of honouring the charter.

Before the year was out he had mustered an army of loyal forces and mercenaries to march upon the rebel Barons. The Pope (Innocent III) sided with the King and excommunicated all who had effected the signing of the Magna Carta document.

The Pope viewed the Barons' actions as a direct assault upon the divine right of the King to rule. Furthermore, in August 1215, he issued a papal bull annulling the charter.

The Barons, for their part, sought help from King Philip of France. Robert de Vere even went to France to offer the 'Dauphin'* the English crown. In return 7,000 French troops landed at Orwell in Suffolk but arrived too late. King John's men had already destroyed Montfitchet Castle. They then went on to take Pleshey, capture de Vere's Castle at Hedingham and force the capitulation of Colchester.

De Vere was now King John's prisoner with his castle and lands confiscated, although unlike Monfitchet, Hedingham Castle was still standing. Within a year everything had changed. Louis, the son of Phillip of France, returned with an army to support the Barons. King John, defeated, fled northwards and died of dysentery in Newark. The new King, Henry III, made peace with the rebels and reissued a revised Magna Carta. The 'rebel' Barons, including Robert de Vere, after swearing loyalty to the crown, were returned to favour and regained their lands.

De Vere died on 25th October 1221 and was buried at Hatfield Priory. His body and effigy were later removed to Hatfield Church where he was reburied. For 500 years successive de Veres played prominent roles in English history. In 1703 Aubrey, the 20th Earl of Oxford, died childless and the title was no more. The estates were broken up and one part was inherited by a linen draper in London, Edward Rigby, whose family had a profound effect on the village of Mistley on the river Stour (see page 78)

Fortunately, in spite of several changes, the guiding principles of the Magna Carta survive to this day.

---

* *The Dauphin of was a title given to the King's eldest son, the heir apparent to the throne of France.*

# HADLEIGH CASTLE

*Hadleigh Castle built on clay*
*Was Hubert's folly locals say.*
*T'will tumble down from its base*
*And like de Burgh fall from grace.*

Hadleigh Castle is over 750 years old. The Castle has seen many comings and goings and many of the characters that crop up in *The Essex Hundred* have visited it. Quite a few have even owned it! The original licence to build was granted to Hubert de Burgh, the Chief Judicial Officer to King John (of Magna Carta fame).

The Castle is now a shadow of its former self. In the great medieval scheme of things it replaced the castle at Rayleigh. The site was considered ideal as it offered magnificent views across the Thames estuary from where any threatened seaborne invasion might come. However, in spite of great effort and expense, the castle's completion simply offered nothing more than a splendid view from the ramparts. It was useless as a deterrent as shot from the primitive artillery of the day could never hit ships entering the Thames. The Castle served no strategic purpose as invaders could easily pass it by thus leaving the defenders wondering what to do next. Furthermore Royalty was little inclined to visit as the journey to Hadleigh from London was difficult both by land and water.

Unfortunately for de Burgh the aftermath of the Magna Carta signing brought much plotting by disgruntled barons. De Burgh was arrested and dismissed from office and ownership of the castle reverted to the King of the day – Henry III.

Over time numerous renovations were undertaken and the Castle suffered from its fair share of shoddy builders. Successive Kings spent a fortune then each in turn lost interest. During the 100 year war with France, King Edward III authorised a complete rebuild and it is said he even lodged there to check up on the workmen. One illustrious occupant was Aubrey de Vere, the 10th Earl of Oxford. He held the post of Constable of the Castle and gave shelter to plotters trying to restore Richard II to the throne after he was deposed (see Silence of Pleshey Castle page 35). Apparently de Vere died at the Castle on 23rd April 1400, St George's day, and is buried in the Hadleigh area.

The long war with France came to an end and the castle went through a succession of owners. There is no record of the castle ever being attacked. The Castle's main enemy was the sea, the salty air and the unstable ground on which it was built. The final demise of the Castle began in the time of Henry VIII.

He showed no interest other than passing the Castle and surrounding land off on three of his wives. However they stayed away too.

Edward VI inherited the Castle from his father but he was a sickly child and died at the age of 15.

The Castle was abandoned and fast becoming a ruin. However during Edward's reign he was persuaded, in 1551, to sell up to Lord Robert Rich of *Leez Priory*. Richard Rich obtained Hadleigh Castle for £700 and was perhaps the original 'Essex wide boy'. He saw a business opportunity and an asset to be stripped. Much of the castle still standing was quickly demolished, with the stone and fittings sold or carted off to one of the many other building projects Lord Rich had in hand at the time. What remained of the castle began to disappear under vegetation. There were regular landslips too. The British landscape painter John Constable came by in 1829 and added the castle to his bulging portfolio of masterpieces. One of Constable's Hadleigh Castle *six footers* hangs in the Tate Gallery.

The Salvation Army acquired the ruins, together with much of the surrounding land, in 1891 when the farm colony was created. After the Second World War it was then handed to the Ministry of Works. Hadleigh Castle is now owned by English Heritage and open to the public with free entry. In August 2008 the area surrounding the castle was selected as the venue for the 2012 Olympic Mountain Biking event.

# DOG OF WAR

*'Giovanni Acuto' the Italians called him.*
*Learned his trade with The Black Prince in France.*
*Thought by Chaucer 'a gentle and courteous man',*
*The 'Diabolical Englishman' led Italy a dance.*

Sir John Hawkwood was, if not the original, then certainly the most famous, and most feared, soldier of fortune in late Middle Age Italy. Born about 1320 in Sible Hedingham, he was the second of three sons of a tanner and minor landowner.

The Hundred Years War with France was a magnet that attracted many young men to seek fame and fortune, John Hawkwood was one of them. He learned his trade fighting with the Black Prince at Poitiers. He became a brilliant tactician and commander who looked after his men and was knighted for his loyalty to the King.

The temporary peace after the treaty of Brétigny meant Hawkwood was left at a loose end. All he knew was war and it was as much about looting as about winning. Being the younger son he had nothing to go back to in England. With thousands of other mercenaries in the same position, he drifted south through France.

Having seen how easy it was to extract money from poorly defended villages, in return for protection organised groups of mercenaries laid siege to the town of Pont-Saint-Esprit. Having decimated the town they turned to nearby Avignon, the seat of the Pope. Hawkwood's career as a 'Condottiere,' in modern terms 'gun for hire,' began here. Pope Innocent VI, fearing an all out attack, paid the leaders, one of them Hawkwood, to take their mercenaries and go to Italy.

Chaucer, who had met Hawkwood, wrote in his Prologue to the Canterbury Tales *of "a verray, parfit gentil knyght"* who *"loved chivalrie, trouthe and honour, fredom and curtesie."* These were not characteristics that many in Italy would recognise in the man they would come to know as Giovanni Acuto, the *'Diabolical Englishman'.*

Many Italian city-states such as Milan, Florence, Pisa and Sienna were vying with each other for supremacy, all fearing attack in one form or another. It was here in northern Italy that Hawkwood's 'White Company' became the most efficient, ruthless and feared force ever. They would work to contracts, negotiated by Hawkwood, for the highest bidder. After putting whole towns under occupation they would purposely destroy harvests to ensure starvation if that was what their paymasters wanted. Terror was their main weapon but if there was no money forthcoming they would burn everything.

In 1377 at Cesena, near Rimini, Hawkwood's mercenaries cold bloodedly murdered as many as 5,000 inhabitants in a savagely organised act of reprisal on the orders of Pope Gregory. The same year, at the age of 57, Hawkwood married the seventeen year old Donnina, daughter of Bernabo Visconti the ruthless ruler of Milan. The alliance with Milan did not last since there was no loyalty from the mercenaries if a better offer came along. And a better offer did come, from Florence. He had fought against the Florentines in the past, now he was hired to protect them and to attack their enemies.

Hawkwood's cold and calculating ruthlessness earned him the title of *The Diabolical Englishman* yet he became a hero in Florence. Giovanni Acuto (Acuto was the nearest the Italians could get to saying Hawkwood) was honoured by the grateful city. His image, in a fresco by Paulo Uccello, adorns the east nave of Florence Cathedral.

He died in 1394 and his remains were transferred to his hometown of Sible Hedingham for burial.

# ONE NIGHT IN BOXTED

*King Edward III had come to nearby Colchester's estate*
*And official records show he entered by the Balkerne gate.*
*Yet he left almost immediately so what was going on?*
*Local dignitaries waited patiently, but the King had gone.*

On the 30th September 1994 the Russian Presidential jet was carrying the first democratically elected Russian leader landed on the west Coast of the Irish Republic. Boris Yeltsin had planned a stopover at Shannon Airport. The red carpet had been rolled out. Waiting on the tarmac to greet Mr Yeltsin was the Irish Prime Minister Albert Reynolds, his wife, two ministers, a group of Irish MPs, an honour guard, a military band and a delegation from the Russian embassy. The plane came to a halt and the group waited – and waited. After an hour a message was handed out that Boris Yeltsin was too tired or too ill to get off the plane. The planned meeting and subsequent lavish state dinner were cancelled. Whilst all the diplomatic niceties were observed it was commonly believed that the Russian president was too drunk to meet anyone.

600 years earlier a similar incident was played out that involved all civic leaders of medieval Colchester. Edward III was the King of England. He spent much of his reign fighting the French during the course of the 100 years war but when not at war he promoted English as the national language and oversaw reforms to the legal system. Treason was also made an offence for the first time during his kingship.

In 1354 there was a truce between the English and the French. When the weather was better and the days longer, the King travelled around the country with his mobile court, the Chancery, trying to resolve some of the more intractable local disputes.

The town of Colchester had been involved in a long dispute with Lionel de Bradenhan, the Lord of Langenhoe Manor. Bradenhan was described as an Essex gentleman but his actions were anything but gentlemanly. His army had besieged the town, ambushing officials attempting to travel in or out, and demanded ransom when they fell into his hands. He had also plundered the oyster beds on the river Colne.

Lionel de Bradenhan was an absolute tyrant. He broke open the town gaol, blocked local water-courses and interfered with the duties of the local coroner. He was certainly one reason for the King to come to Colchester. Although the date cannot be confirmed it was probably at Michaelmas (29th September 1354). It is known that the 'Law Hundred' - or Court of the Borough - was usually held on this day.

Edward would probably have travelled from London, stopping overnight at the Royal Manor at Writtle, before moving on to Colchester. With the King expected all the town dignitaries were in attendance. Waiting close to the Balkerne Gate a ceremonial guard was lined up. Arrangements for suitable lodging would have been made and a sumptuous feast prepared. Onlookers jostled for the best position to see the King.

Midday arrived and suddenly there was a great commotion. The King was seen entering through the Balkerne Gate. However his face could not be seen through the phalanx of bodyguards, soldiers and court officials. The King appeared to come closer to the reception committee but then vanished. That was it! The Civic leaders of Colchester waited and waited. Where was the King? Then word came that the King was not coming and had never intended to come to Colchester in the first place and the court should proceed without him.

Legend has it that Edward came to Colchester on the date in question but for a completely different motive. He had absolutely no intention of presiding over the law hundred. Elements of the King's Court were sent into Colchester, creating confusion. Edward himself had gone straight from Writtle to Boxted Hall, arriving late afternoon accompanied only by his personal bodyguard.

Boxted Hall was the family home of Peter de Boxted, Sheriff of Essex. His duties meant regular absences from his estate on the King's business sometimes accompanied by his wife, Lady Sybil. At the time of their marriage Sybil, a vivacious, attractive girl who moved well in aristocratic circles, was young enough to be Peter's granddaughter. On one of their visits to the Royal Court she was 'noticed' by the King.

At Michaelmas, 29th September 1354, Peter de Boxted was away on official business; Lady Sybil was at home alone in Boxted Hall, and the King was certainly missing from his duties in Colchester.

Sybil may have got her man for one night in Boxted but Colchester's leading citizens, much like the Irish Prime Minister all those years later, had definitely been stood up!

# THREE DAYS THAT SHOOK THE KINGDOM

*Thomas Brampton, King Richard's tax collector*
*Empowered to deal harshly with any objector.*
*Entered Brentwood with his clerks in tow,*
*Any waiver requests would be met with a firm NO!*

In May 1381 England was recovering from the 'Black Death' a plague that killed between one third and half of the population. At the same time the nation was embroiled with its '100 years' war with France. The war was not going well and was expensive. The majority of the army overseas had not been paid for months. The decline in population had substantially reduced tax revenues and put a severe strain on the feudal system that effectively obliged labourers to work for a specific manorial Lord in perpetuity. There was now a labour shortage and in many cases men simply left their manors to find work elsewhere for better wages and conditions.

Parliament was determined to raise money. Five years earlier it had introduced the first Poll Tax. This head tax had applied to almost everyone over the age of 14. A second poll tax was levied in 1379 and, in 1380, a third charging one shilling, or 3 groats (5p), on all people over the age of 16. It was hoped that the richer elements in society would help the poor; piously expressed at the time as *'the strong might aid the weak'*. This was the case in some areas but in many places the tax was a heavy burden.

This latest tax managed to antagonise nearly everyone and led to widespread evasion. Official population figures for Essex of 1381 showed a dramatic decrease in population of 35 – 40% from the previously recorded figure. This downward adjustment of the population figures was achieved with the connivance of civic leaders who simply understated the local population on their returns.

Parliament became suspicious and sent commissioners to check on the numbers of people liable to pay the tax. On 30th May 1381 tax commissioners, headed by John Brampton, arrived in Brentwood to conduct enquiries for the Barstable Hundred. Holding court close to the Thomas à Becket Chapel*, the commissioners were suddenly confronted by hundreds of angry armed men led by Thomas Baker from Fobbing. Brampton and his court took fright and fled back to London with his entourage.

Three days later on Whit Sunday 2nd June, a High Court Judge, Sir Robert Belknap, arrived with the task of restoring order and resuming the enquiry. Belknap was not a good choice, being very unpopular.

The mob had now grown to thousands and the Judge's 'hard man' approach only inflamed them further.

Riot ensued. Belknap was manhandled then stripped and made to swear an oath on the bible. He was lucky to escape with his life. Three of his clerks were not so fortunate. They were seized and beheaded, as were some local jurors accused of collaborating. Their heads were put on poles for all to see. All the court records were then burnt in a huge bonfire. The incident was a catalyst that sparked the 'Peasants or Great Revolt' in Essex.

Almost immediately attacks took place all over the County, especially on those associated with Parliament. As always, criminals and other malcontents used the opportunity to loot and burn and settle scores.

The Essex rebels joined with those of Kent, who were led by Wat Tyler, and laid siege to London. The government of Richard II was nearly toppled after the rebels captured the Tower of London, destroyed the Savoy, and in the process, killed the Chancellor and The Treasurer.

Two weeks after it all began on 15th June, Richard II confronted the rebels at Smithfield. Their leader Wat Tyler, who was worse the wear for drink whilst attempting to speak with the King, died after skirmishing with William Walworth the Mayor of London. The young King Richard, only 14 years old, faced the crowd and won them over with promises of fair treatment and claims on their loyalty. The Revolt was effectively over. Wat Tyler is remembered today as a hero of the people and is commemorated in Pitsea by the 'Wat Tyler Country Park'.

*The remains of Thomas à Becket Chapel are in Brentwood High Street. It was a popular stopping point for pilgrims travelling south on their way to Canterbury in the middle ages.*

# RETRIBUTION

*Essex was where 'The whole madness first sprang'*
*So it was only natural the ringleaders would hang.*
*The King lodged at Writtle where his edicts flowed*
*For seven days, in a torrent that never slowed.*

Following the death of Wat Tyler, and the peaceful dispersal of his followers at Smithfield, King Richard II moved swiftly to impose his authority.

Elements of the rebellion were still active in the country. In Essex a sizeable rebel group that had massed near Billericay was confronted and defeated by forces loyal to the King. As the countryside was secured the King and his court moved from London to Havering and on to Chelmsford. From 1st July until 6th July 1381 the King lodged in his manor house* at Writtle.

For seven days Writtle became the seat of Government. Edicts and proclamations were produced almost non-stop and messengers carried them to all corners of the Kingdom. Their substance was that the rebellion was over and the only lawful authority was the King or his appointees. Furthermore, any promises made to the rebels earlier were withdrawn as they had been made 'under duress'. To quash any hopes that lingered of new found freedoms Richard II stated *"Villeins ye are still and villeins ye shall remain".* **

Following the death of the Chief Justice Sir John Cavendish, killed by the rebels, the King appointed Sir Robert Tresilian. He set up court in Chelmsford with the purpose of bringing the instigators of the revolt to justice. Delegations of 'rebels' came to Chelmsford begging for mercy. Tresilian promised to spare their lives if the ringleaders were named. Over 145 rebel leaders were identified. No mercy was shown those who were caught. After a short trial they were executed and their property confiscated. Included in these was Thomas Baker from Fobbing.

Although the status quo returned there was no doubt the rebellion had rocked the establishment to its core. The Chancellor, the Chief Justice and the Treasurer had been killed. Several Royal lodges and 'Official' buildings had been looted then burned and most of the local records had been destroyed along with them.

In a final twist Parliament declared a general amnesty to all rebels still at large on 14 December 1381.

*\* Formerly King John's Palace and now the site of Writtle College.*
*\*\*The word Villien is derived from the French or Latin villanus, meaning serf or peasant, someone who is tied to the land and manor.*

# THE SILENCE OF PLESHEY CASTLE

*Ghosts of long dead Dukes and Earls*
*Reflect on dark deeds of jealous Kings*
*Atop the mound; all that remains,*
*Of Pleshey's once resplendent halls.*

The village of Pleshey lies in the parish of High Easter, between Chelmsford and Dunmow. It was given to Geoffrey de Mandeville by William the Conqueror as reward for his support at the battle of Hastings. As High Constable of England he became one of the most powerful men in Essex with Pleshey Castle as his family seat. Initially the castle would have been a typical Norman earthwork, motte and bailey with wooden palisades and tower. By the end of the twelfth century it was a stone built castle, the home of Geoffrey's grandson, Geoffrey III, Earl of Essex.

In 1215 forces loyal to King John in his battles with the Barons over the Magna Carta besieged Pleshey. De Mandeville surrendered and by doing so ensured that his castle was not destroyed, as had happened to Montfitchet castle at Stansted.

By the 14th century the castle had passed, through inheritance, to Eleanor de Bohun. When she married Thomas of Woodstock, Duke of Gloucester and the youngest son of Edward III, the castle became their home. Gloucester was also uncle to, and one of the guardians of, the young King Richard II. On reaching maturity Richard tired of the interference of his guardians, particularly Gloucester. And so began, in 1397, one of the most infamous events in the history of Pleshey.

Richard, while staying at his house in Havering-Atte-Bower, now part of Romford, paid an allegedly friendly, but unexpected, visit to his uncle at Pleshey. Welcomed, he dined there and then persuaded Gloucester to accompany him to London for a meeting the next day with his other uncles, York and Lancaster. They set off and on reaching Stratford the King rode on ahead leaving his uncle to be ambushed by the Earl Marshal and a troop of men. Gloucester was arrested *'in the King's name,'* taken to the Thames and put aboard a ship bound for Calais. He was declared a traitor and all his lands confiscated to the crown. When requests for his return to face trial were sent to Calais the reply came back that Gloucester had died in prison. How he died was never disclosed but an inquisition set up after the accession of King Henry IV found; *"...that he had been fraudulently and wickedly smothered, by the king's orders at Calais."* This episode in the life of Pleshey is immortalised by William Shakespeare in his play, Richard the Second, where he uses it as the trigger for Henry (Bolingbroke) to depose Richard and seize the crown.

This was in 1399. Henry decreed that all of Gloucester's possessions, including Pleshey, were restored to his widow Eleanor. Later that year Richard met his demise. Deposed as a tyrant he was imprisoned in Pontefract Castle, Yorkshire, where he died, most probably from starvation.

Today Pleshey castle is no more. The mound or motte, some fifteen metres in height and one of the largest in England, remains, as does evidence of the inner and outer baileys that once contained the limits of the village.

*Henry V died leaving widow Catherine*
*And baby son Henry to reign as king.*
*Owen Tudor then made Catherine his wife*
*Of lowly rank he was the love of her life.*

**"The King is dead! Long live the King!**

If this cry was heard in London in September 1422, the King in question would have been Henry V who, on 31 August 1422, had died suddenly of a mysterious illness in France. He left a young widow, Catherine de Valois, and his successor the nine month old Henry VI.

Catherine, still a young woman, in time fell in love, secretly married and had four children with a commoner, Owen Tudor. When their secret became known the council of young Henry's advisers were furious. The liaison was one thing but children and a legal marriage was out of the question for the mother of the King.

Owen Tudor fled to Wales; Catherine to Bermondsey Abbey, their children, probably at the behest of their half brother the King, were sent to Barking Abbey. There, under the Abbess Katherine de la Pole, they were educated as royalty. One of the children, Edmund was later created earl of Richmond and married Margaret Beaufort. Their only son Henry, born shortly after his father died , grew up to become the first Tudor King of England, Henry VII.

The Abbey had a long association with royalty. Founded in 666 by Erkenwald for his sister Ethelburga, it was endowed with land and property by many East Saxon Princes. Destroyed by Vikings in 870, it was rebuilt a hundred years later as a royal foundation with the appointment of each Abbess being the prerogative of the King.

The growing importance of the Abbey was shown when William the Conqueror, at the end of 1066, established his court there while the Tower of London was being built. Under continued royal patronage successive Abbesses included Queens, Princesses or were drawn from the ranks of favoured nobility. The Abbess held precedence over all other Abbesses. As the power of the church grew Barking Abbey's fortunes flourished. The manors that were owned by the Abbey included Barking, Dagenham, Warley, Leaden Roding, Ingatestone, Hockley, Tollesbury and many others.

In 1539 however the Abbey fell victim to Henry VIII's battle with the Catholic Church (see page 44, Dissolution) and was surrendered to William Petrie, the Royal Commissioner. (During this transaction Petrie acquired the Abbey's manor of Ingatestone where his family live to this day.)

After 1540 the Abbey buildings were demolished for building materials and for nearly four hundred years the site was virtually a quarry. In 1910 excavations of the original site were begun and today the ruins of the Abbey and St Margaret's Churchyard may be seen in a conservation area which is open to the Public.

**Curfew Tower Barking Abbey**

# The Dunmow Flitch

*'You shall swear by the Custom of our Confession*
*That you never made any Nuptial Transgression'*
*'For this is our Custom at Dunmow well known*
*Though the sport be ours, the bacon's your own.'*

Over nine hundred years ago Reginald Fitzwalter and his wife decided that their marriage lasting a year and a day without regrets was deserving of recognition. Disguising themselves in humble clothing they approached the Augustinian Prior to bless their union. Afterwards Fitzwalter revealed his identity as Lord of the Manor and in gratitude gave the priory some land. The gift was conditional on a flitch, or side, of bacon being awarded annually to a couple who could demonstrate a similar devotion. This, legend would have it, is how, in 1104, the 'Dunmow Flitch' was born.

The modern Trials, held every leap year, take place in Great Dunmow in a court with a presiding Judge. Counsel represents the claimants who must be married for a year and a day. Opposing counsel appears for the donors of the Flitch of Bacon. A Jury of six maidens and six bachelors has to be persuaded. A Clerk records the proceedings with an Usher keeping order.

Successful couples are carried shoulder high in the ancient Flitch Chair to the Market Place where they take the oath kneeling on pointed stones. The unsuccessful couples walk behind and receive a consolation prize of gammon.

The Dunmow Flitch trials were a widely known tradition in the fourteenth century since they are mentioned by William Langland in his book, 'The Vision of Piers Plowman', in 1362. The first recorded winner of a Flitch though was Richard Wright of Norwich in 1445.

After the dissolution of the Monasteries by Henry VIII the custom seems to have lapsed until the Lord of the Manor briefly revived it in the eighteenth century. Thomas Shakeshaft and his wife, who won the flitch in 1751, immediately cut it up and sold it piecemeal to the crowd. The Lord of the Manor perhaps understandably distressed by this, lost interest and the ceremony lapsed again.

The trials were revived again around 1855 as a civic event, mainly through the efforts of Harrison Ainsworth* who, in 1854, wrote a very popular book entitled, 'The Flitch of Bacon or The Custom of Dunmow'. In this Ainsworth tells of the publican of 'The Flitch of Bacon' trying to win the Flitch by marrying a succession of wives in order to find a perfect one. Since then the event has only been interrupted by the two wars, although since World War Two the annual event has given way to trials being held four-yearly on the leap year.

*In 1834 Harrison Ainsworth also wrote 'Rookwood' which was responsible for some of the myth surrounding Dick Turpin. (See page 68, Stand and Deliver)*

**The Prize Winning Flitch**

# LOYAL SUBJECT
## HENRY MARNEY

*On Bosworth's bloody field Henry Marney made his name.*
*Richard III had lost the crown to which Henry VII now laid claim.*

The Marneys had lived in Layer Marney for nearly three hundred years before Henry was born in 1447. They had come to England in the wake of William the Conqueror. The family was known to be resident in Layer Marney in 1166, some hundred years after the Battle of Hastings. By 1414 the family had a certain status in the county since Henry's grandfather William had become Sheriff of Essex.

Henry Marney was a loyal supporter of Henry Tudor in the wars of the roses. He fought at the battles of Stoke and Bosworth Field and was knighted after the resounding defeat of Perkin Warbeck and his Cornish rebels at Blackheath in 1497.

The Wars of the Roses were effectively ended at Bosworth. Richard III had been killed, his forces routed and Henry Tudor was proclaimed King in the field. On being crowned, Henry VII did not forget his supporters. Henry Marney was appointed to the Privy Council. He was a friend, confidante and guide to the King and remained a Privy Councillor when the King died, serving his son, Henry VIII.

Serving Henry VIII, Marney became Knight of the Bath; Lord Privy Seal; Vice Chamberlain of the Household; Chancellor of the Duchy of Lancaster; Captain of the Yoemen of the Guard and was eventually created Lord Marney.

Marney planned to build a grand house at Layer Marney. Modelled upon Wolsey's Hampton Court Palace it was to be even more magnificent. Unfortunately he died in 1523 leaving his son, Lord Marney II, to complete the building. He also died suddenly two years later, leaving a partly rebuilt Church of St Mary the Virgin, a stable block, the front side of the Courtyard Palace and the main house not started. Provision in both their wills allowed for the church to be completed. Built in the perpendicular style of locally made Tudor brick, it contains a mural of St Christopher dated circa 1520 and the tombs of father and son, the first and last Lords Marney.

John Marney left two daughters who sold the estate in 1533 to Sir Brian Tuke, High Sheriff of Essex. His son George added the spectacular eight storey, four turreted Gatehouse – now at eighty feet the tallest Tudor gatehouse in the country.

Henry Marney's dream house was never built and the building became known as Layer Marney Tower. George Tuke died in 1577. Two years later his widow entertained Queen Elizabeth I for two days. The Queen probably stayed in what is now the billiard room on the ground floor.

The estate then passed through many hands and had been almost continuously occupied for generations. It was considerably damaged in the Great Earthquake of 1884, (see page122) though it was repaired soon afterwards. In 1959 the house came into the possession of the Charrington Family who have been in residence since then.

Today the house and gardens are open to the public and remain a lasting memorial to Tudor times and the part that Henry Marney played in them.

# To Marry a King

*Rochford 100 golf course, so serene.*
*The thwack! Of golf balls on the green.*
*A girl called Anne was born to be Queen*
*Here in Rochford Hall, to Thomas Boleyn.*

Rochford has two visible reminders of the town's part in the saga of the country's most married King: 'The Anne Boleyn' pub, named after Rochford's most famous daughter, and 'Rochford Hundred Golf Club', which occupies her one time family home, Rochford Hall.

The Manor of Rochford has passed through many hands since its $12^{th}$ century association with the De Rochford family. Acquired by Thomas Boleyn in the early fifteen hundreds it became the Boleyn family home in 1525 when he was given the title Viscount Rochford. Some said this was because his eldest daughter Mary had been Henry VIII's mistress. They may be right since the highly educated Boleyn was also ruthlessly ambitious.

Thomas had three children, George, Mary and Anne - they were probably all born at the family seat, Blickling Hall in Norfolk , between 1499 and 1507.

The Boleyn's fortunes took a setback when Henry tired of Mary but looked up when he met sister Anne and fell madly in love. The King often hunted in the forests around Rochford and frequently visited Anne at Rochford Hall. Thomas who saw it as increasing his prestige and power at court feverishly encouraged the match.

Settling for nothing less than marriage, Anne became Queen. She was pregnant when they married in 1533 and in September gave birth to the future Queen Elizabeth. She had many enemies at court and politically motivated plots and intrigues against her abounded. These, coupled with her inability to produce a son and heir, were to be her downfall.

In time Henry's attentions wandered and when Jane Seymour came on the scene, and still no son, Anne had to go. On trumped up charges she was accused of treason and adultery with her brother George among others. Anne's father could do nothing to help her, the King was determined to have his way.

Thomas was forced to preside over the trial of the other five men accused with Anne and George and he condemned them all. He was lucky to escape being caught up in the intrigue himself. Always a loyal and faithful servant of the King, Henry excused him from being involved in the trial of his children. Nevertheless he accepted the verdicts and had to witness their executions.

Mary had earlier been the king's mistress whilst married to Sir William Carey with whom she had two children, Henry and Catherine - there has been speculation, never substantiated, that their father was Henry VIII. Carey died in 1528 and Mary then married Sir William Stafford. Living in quiet retirement at Rochford she inherited the estate on her father's death in 1539. In 1552 her son Henry sold Rochford Hall to Lord Richard Rich who owned Hadleigh Castle and acquired Lees Priory, as well as many other Essex manors, during the *Dissolution (see page 44).*

# TYNDALE'S FRIEND

*At dead of night standing at the quayside*
*Thomas Poyntz awaited the incoming tide*
*At last a small vessel slid in and docked*
*Its secret cargo in chests firmly locked.*

William Tyndale was ordained a priest in 1521. A talented scholar, his ambition was to translate the Latin Bible into English so that people could read it for themselves. They would then not have to accept whatever the clergy told them. This was strictly forbidden in Henry VIII's England. Church leaders such as Cardinal Wolsey, and later Thomas More, vigorously enforced the law.

Tyndale began translating the New Testament but was forced to flee to Worms in Germany where he eventually completed it. In 1526 copies were being read in England, albeit behind closed doors. King Henry's spies were everywhere though and Tyndale had to be very careful. In 1534 he decided to move to Antwerp where he thought he could live safely.

There were many 'English Houses' in Antwerp. Thomas Poyntz, an Essex merchant from North Ockenden, ran one of them. Poyntz was sympathetic to reform and welcomed Tyndale to his house. It was here that Tyndale continued his work, translating and publishing the complete English Bible. They were printed by the thousand.

There was considerable trade between England and Antwerp. Bibles could be shipped hidden in bales of cloth, in barrels or disguised as boxes of legal goods relatively easily. It was a highly risky business. The East Coast ports of England were watched continuously. Merchants such as Poyntz, keen supporters of church reformation, had to be very careful. Shipments were made at dead of night and often to little known places like Purfleet. The contraband then had to be dispersed which was also extremely dangerous.

Seen as a heretic by the church, and not only in England, Tyndale had many enemies. One of these, Henry Phillips, an agent posing as a friend, betrayed him to the authorities. He was arrested and imprisoned in Vilvoorde Castle in what is now Belgium.

The strenuous activities of Poyntz and his family in petitioning Thomas Cromwell and Henry VIII for his release and extradition all failed. After a year and a half, in 1536, Tyndale was taken to the Market Square, tied to a stake and strangled and his body burnt.

Thomas Poyntz, also branded as a heretic by Henry Phillips, was put under house arrest in Antwerp but escaped to England.

Despite the fact that John Poyntz, elder brother to Thomas, was a member of the household of Queen Catherine of Aragon, and had been at 'The Field of the Cloth of Gold' with Henry VIII, on his return Thomas' life was in ruins. As a known heretic he was under surveillance by Henry's spies and his continued involvement in the spreading of the new Bible meant life was very difficult.

Thomas may have felt vindicated when, two years after the death of Tyndale, Henry VIII decreed that Miles Coverdale's English Bible, based largely on Tyndale's translation, must be used in every parish church in the country. Vindicated maybe but the damage was done, his fortunes did not improve. When in 1558 he succeeded to the Manor of North Ockendon on the death of his brother John, he could not afford to live there. He died in 1562 and is buried in St Dunstans in the West, in Fleet Street, London.

North Ockendon's Church of St Mary Magdelene lies next to the site of the old Manor House. In its Poyntz Chapel, dedicated in the will of John Poyntz to 'Our Lady', the family are remembered. Thomas' son Sir Gabriel Poyntz, twice Lord Lieutenant of Essex under Elizabeth I, restored the family fortunes. He commissioned the tomb effigies of himself and his wife and also a series of wall tablets commemorating his ancestors, including Thomas, which survive today. The church also boasts the Poyntz Singers which is the present day church choir.

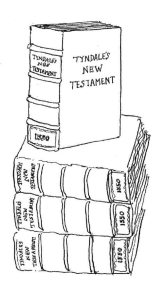

# DISSOLUTION

*The King had proclaimed that monasteries would be closed,*
*All their assets confiscated or otherwise disposed.*

After polling 5,000 people in 2005, BBC's History Magazine nominated Richard Riche as the third worst Briton of the last 1,000 years. He was number one for the 16th century.

Riche made his Baronial seat at Leez Priory close to Felsted in Essex. Originally this was an Augustinian monastery occupying land by the river Ter. It was built by Sir Ralph Gernon shortly after the Magna Carta was signed. Mr, then Sir, then Lord and finally Baron, Riche was also a great benefactor to the village of Felsted. His charitable foundations there include Felsted School where today he is commemorated by its 'Lord Riche Hall', a purpose built dining room and function area.

Riche was one of the sixteenth century's greatest survivors. He held high office throughout the reign of Henry VIII, Edward VI, Queen Mary and into Elizabeth's time. The young Queen Elizabeth I was even a guest at his home. In these turbulent times many of his peers found their way to the block or were burnt at the stake. Riche skilfully managed to stay on the right side of the reigning monarch at all times. He had the knack of knowing when to take a low profile. Not only did he survive he also became exceedingly wealthy.

Riche's career was meteoric by the standards of the day. In short succession, and before the age of 40, he was an MP for Colchester, Solicitor General and most rewarding of all, Chancellor of the Court of Augmentations. Henry VIII had set up this court with the express purpose of dissolving the monasteries. Following the split with Papacy he needed to confirm himself as head of the Church in England and break the power of the church once and for all.

As a result the crown acquired all monastic lands, amounting in total to approximately one third of the country. The problem for Henry was that he did not have the resources to manage these acquisitions. Richard Riche however was in the right place at the right time. As the head of the court he persuaded the King to let him organise the dissolution and to dispose of estates the crown didn't want. In this way many properties that passed though the Chancellor's office '*stuck to his hands*'.

During his lifetime Richard Riche acquired at least 100 manors in Essex alone, including Leez Priory, most of Rochford, Fyfield, large areas of present-day Thurrock and Hadleigh Castle.

When Henry VIII died in 1547 his son Edward VI succeeded him. Edward was 10 years old and a sickly child. Baron Riche promptly retired and set about building a huge mansion at Leez Priory. He had acquired the Priory a decade earlier and, like many others, under dubious circumstances.

The procedure was that a King's agent would visit the monastery in question to value it and report back to the officials at the Court of Augmentation. Sometimes this is what was done. At other times gangs of thugs might be sent along to ensure that a desired valuation was arrived at. They also ensured that acquisitions took place according to a timetable dictated by the new owner, in this case Chancellor Riche!

Throughout his career Richard Riche had been adept at changing sides. He had been complicit in garnering evidence against any opponents of the Monarch. His testimony more than once resulted in executions. He is even alleged to have personally tortured a religious reformer, Anne Askew, before she was burnt at the stake. On the death of King Edward at the age 16, Baron Riche came out of retirement. Sensing change, and with it opportunity, he involved himself in the succession.

Mary, daughter of Catherine of Aragon, Henry VIII's first wife, eventually took the throne. A devout catholic, Mary promptly set about undoing many of Edward's Protestant reforms. She pursued her religious convictions with zeal. Over 250 heretics were burnt at the stake during her rule. All the time Robert Riche was by her side.

When Queen Elizabeth succeeded Queen Mary, yet again Baron Riche changed his allegiance. Now approaching 70, quite an achievement in the 16th century, he had mellowed. He began his charitable work perhaps as atonement for previous sins. On one of her Royal Progressions Queen Elizabeth stayed at Leez for five days, which was unusually long and would have been enormously expensive for the host. Happily for Riche he could comfortably afford it.

Baron Riche died in Rochford on 12th June 1567 and was buried in Felsted. Whether he deserves the BBC 'accolade' is a matter for the reader to judge.

# PIE POWDER COURT SITTING

*'The charge, false weight and measures my lord*
*We have a witness here who will testify to fraud'.*

In spite of all the intrigue and plotting surrounding Queen Elizabeth I and threats to the nation from abroad, most of the population tried, as far as possible, to carry on with their lives and businesses as normal.

For some people normal business was sharp practice, fraud and deception. For others their job was to apprehend cheats, prosecute them and in general to see justice done.

In 1566 Richard Asser found himself before what was known as the 'Pie Powder' Court in the Moot Hall in Maldon. The term 'Pie Powder' is assumed to have been derived from the 'Old' French *pieds poudreux,* a term that referred to the dusty feet of travelling traders. The courts had unlimited jurisdiction for all events taking place in the market, including disputes between traders, theft and acts of violence. According to William Blackstone in his *Commentaries on the Laws of England,* published in the 1760s, *"They existed because of the necessity for speedy justice over people who were not permanent residents of the place where the market was held".*

Richard Asser was one such travelling salesman who traded in a number of Essex markets. He was before the court after being discovered using false weights and measures. Court records of the day also showed that three shoemakers and two saddlers appeared, charged with displaying goods of poor quality.

As a punishment the sale items were seized, valued and sold. The money realised was divided into thirds and shared between the market inspectors, the court and the poor. The false weights and measures likewise would have been confiscated. The rogue trader, Richard Asser, would probably have suffered an additional fine and possibly a spell in the stocks.

Pie Powder courts first started 200 years before Mr Asser's time. The authority to convene the courts was written into the Royal charters, which enabled the local Lord of the Manor to hold markets on his lands.

The last known sitting of a Pie Powder Court was in Bristol in 1870, although the rights to hold them were not taken off the statute book until 1977. Today National trading standards are enshrined in law. Market disputes fall within the jurisdiction of the local authority and are overseen by Market Inspectors, backed up by the Police and local Magistrates courts as necessary.

# HARBINGERS AT HARLOW

*The trumpeters sounded and pealing church bells*
*Announced the arrival of Good Bess, their Queen.*
*Outriders in scarlet and gold spangled livery*
*Heralded such sights before never seen.*

In an age without mass communication Queen Elizabeth I cultivated the goodwill of her subjects by means of annual 'progressions'. These tours of different parts of the country were principally designed to allow her to see, and be seen by, her people. They generally took place during the summer months and involved the whole court, as many as five hundred people on the move for weeks at a time.

On three of these progressions through Essex, in September 1571, August 1576 and in July 1578, Elisabeth stayed at Mark Hall in Latton, the home of James Altham, Sheriff of Essex, and his wife Lady Mary Judd. It was an honour to be chosen, albeit an expensive one, though their standing in the community would be enhanced considerably. To be chosen three times indicates that they were very wealthy.

Weeks before the intended visit royal inspectors called *'harbingers'* would be sent to the hosts to ensure that their accommodation was fit for the Queen. Meeting their standards could mean a lot of work and expense, from rearranging furniture to re-decorating or even re-building if things were not to their liking. The *'harbingers'* arrival brought panic, followed by frenzied activity to meet their demands. Sometimes they could mean financial hardship or even ruin if the visit went badly. Hence the modern day phrase, *'harbingers of doom'*.

As the progression approached Mark Hall people from the villages of Latton, Harlow, Nettleswell and Parndon would have gathered to see their Queen. It would have been a grand and colourful sight; heralds followed by trumpeters, their fanfares competing with cheering and the peal of bells from St Mary-at-Latton. The court would levy fines if the bells were not rung for the Queen. Finally Elizabeth would ride up in her finery to be greeted by her hosts and local dignitaries. Speeches would be made and gifts exchanged, in all there would be something of a carnival atmosphere.

Mark Hall was not big enough to accommodate the royal party. The overflow guests were put up in Latton Hall, also owned by the Althams, in local Inns or in tents. All however expected to be fed at the host's expense.

Mark Hall is remembered in Harlow today by two districts bearing the name, Mark Hall North and Mark Hall South. Most of the Hall was burned down in 1947. The surviving wing, which became a primary school, was demolished in 1960. The Church of St Mary-at-Latton, lying quite close to the Mark Hall site, contains a memorial to James Altham and Mary Judd.

Queen Elizabeth's liking for Essex is shown by the fact that she also stayed at Leez Priory as the guest of Lord Richard Riche who had become one of the wealthiest men in the country (see page 44, Dissolution).

# JUST MAD ABOUT SAFFRON

*As far as the eye could see saffron grew,*
*Shining purple and white in the morning dew.*

It is generally accepted that the word saffron is derived from the Arabic Za'faran. Saffron is taken from the stigma of the saffron crocus, *Crocus Sativus*. In normal conditions it flowers between September and November. It was a highly prized commodity used for flavouring, dyeing and medicinal purposes and buyers would travel great distances to acquire it.

The plant was introduced into Essex during Norman times. Walden was an ideal place to grow such a crop as the soil was good and the climate favourable. Although not much saffron was actually grown in the confines of Walden, the town became the centre of the commerce associated with it. Soon Walden became known as Chipping (meaning market) Walden.

Wool was a major product in England and the demand for saffron dye was enormous, and the spice trade flourished. In the plant's honour, the town's name was changed to Saffron Walden. The earliest documented evidence of this is 1582. There may also have been a regal connection with the name change. Sir Thomas Smith, a Walden man by birth, was Secretary of State to Queen Elizabeth I.

As with all industries there are periodic ups and downs. Sir Thomas Smith sought to revive the fortunes of the town, perhaps by suggesting a name change as a marketing ploy. It could be said in modern parlance that it was an early form of corporate re-branding!

The workers who harvested the crop were known as *Crokers*. Each flower had three stigmas which had to be plucked by hand. 75,000 flowers were needed to produce one pound of spice.

The market for local saffron gradually declined with cheaper foreign alternatives available and a growing reluctance to use it for medicinal purposes. The final nail in its coffin was the collapse of the English woollen industry in the 1700s. However the name Saffron Walden lives on - with no plans to change it in the near future as far as we know.

# A Weak and Feeble Woman

*'I know I have the body of a weak and feeble woman,'*
*the nobles looked on as the Queen began,*
*And all those kneeling rose as one to stand,*
*'But I have the heart and stomach of a king of England.'*

The words, *'I know I have the body of a weak and feeble woman,'* were spoken by Queen Elizabeth I on a windswept field in West Tilbury on the 9th August 1588. These were perhaps the most memorable and inspirational words ever recorded by a monarch of England when the kingdom was under threat. That this occurred in Essex only shows the strategic importance of the county. A day earlier the Queen arrived at Tilbury Fort travelling by royal barge from London. With her entourage she made her way to Saffron Gardens, just south of Horndon-on-the-Hill, where she spent the night. The following day Elizabeth headed for the great military camp set up adjacent to the present day *Gunn Hill* farm. Befitting the occasion the Queen rode up, marshal's baton in her hand, clad in white armour on a grey charger. The Earls of Essex and Leicester held the bridle-rein. Assembled were more than 20,000 soldiers standing by to repel any land invasion unleashed from Armada ships.

The Queen spoke with an unmatched passion. *'Let tyrants fear - I come amongst you, not for recreation or sport'* and famously offered *'in the midst and heat of the battle, to live or die amongst you all.'* Angrily the Queen poured scorn on the Papal forces that would dare invade England. To strengthen defences a boom had been constructed across the Thames between Gravesend and Tilbury to prevent enemy vessels making up- stream to London. Additionally the watch ships *Victory* and *Lyon* patrolled at strategic points further down the estuary to intercept suspicious craft. The church towers at Fobbing and Leigh on Sea served as look out points with their beacon turrets ready to be fired if invaders were spotted. Leigh fishermen were conscripted as waterborne messengers.

Ironically the great speech made by Queen Elizabeth took place when much of the threat from the Spanish had been neutralised. Originally the Armada set sail from Lisbon with 130 ships and some 30,000 men in early July. However the English, through a combination of superior intelligence, better ships and seamanship, together with favourable weather and good luck saw the defeat of the Armada by July 29th. As the prospect of invasion receded most of the troops at Tilbury were withdrawn in late August. The remnants of the Armada finally limped home in mid-September, battered by gales, having lost half the fleet and most of its men.

# THE FATHER OF ENGLISH MUSIC
## IN STONDON MASSEY

*'William Byrd was a musical phenomenon*
*hroughout Europe acknowledged supreme.*
*Without him musicians, from Elgar to Elton,*
*Would not have known where to begin.'*

William Byrd's lifetime spanned the reign of five monarchs, Henry VIII, Edward VI, Mary, Elizabeth I and James I. This was a period of considerable turmoil especially if, like Byrd, one was a Roman Catholic. He is acknowledged as one of the great masters of the late renaissance and by some as the greatest English composer ever.

Brought to the attention of Queen Elizabeth, he accepted a position in the Royal Chapel. A known Catholic in a vehemently Protestant England, he was always discrete. His loyalty to the crown was never in question and he enjoyed the favour of the Queen. Elizabeth awarded him, jointly with Thomas Tallis his one time teacher, the monopoly on music publishing. That he was allowed to keep this, even after the death of Tallis is a measure of his status.

He wrote a great deal of sacred songs in Latin which was banned. They could only be performed in secret Catholic services held in private residences. These were frequently held in Ingatestone Hall, the seat of the Petrie family. Sir John Petrie, Byrd's wealthiest patron, Sheriff of Essex and First Lord of Writtle, was also a Roman Catholic. Religion of choice, it would seem, could be followed as long as it wasn't obvious.

After retiring from the Royal Chapel at the age of fifty Byrd went to live in Stondon Massey, a small village close to Ingatestone. A further factor in his choice of Stondon Massey may have been that it was one of three parishes in that part of Essex where Roman Catholicism was fairly strong. Services were held, albeit behind closed doors, in many private houses throughout the Elizabethan years of persecution.

Byrd acquired Stondon Place in 1593 where he lived until his death thirty years later. It has been said that during this period he composed some of his finest music. The previous owner of the house, William Shelley, a suspect in the Throckmorton plot to overthrow Elizabeth, was sentenced to death and his estates forfeit. He was subsequently reprieved and released in 1596 by which time the Byrd family had taken up residence.

The original Stondon Place, a large farmhouse, was rebuilt in 1770 and again after a fire in 1880. There is no evidence of Byrd having lived and created great music in the village now, only the tranquillity of a rural parish whose population, despite the building of the last thirty years, is still little more than 600.

# TIMELINE

| ESSEX EVENT COMMEMORATED | YEAR | NATIONAL OR INTERNATIONAL EVENT |
|---|---|---|
| | 1603 | *Queen Elizabeth I dies* |
| Harwich granted Royal Charter | 1604 | *William Shakespeare writes Othello* |
| Canvey Dutch Cottage Built | 1618 | *Sir Walter Raleigh is executed* |
| Ninth Family Group Join Mayflower | 1620 | *Pilgrim Fathers leave Plymouth* |
| Death of Billericay Pioneers | 1621 | *James I dies, Charles I is King* |
| Rev Dillingham completes 511 Wedding ceremonies in Sandon near Chelmsford | 1635 | *The speed of the Hackney carriage is set in London at 3mph* |
| Smuggling in Leigh on Sea continues | 1642 | *English Civil War starts* |
| Matthew Hopkins charges Elizabeth Clarke of Manningtree with Witchcraft | 1644 | *Abel Tasman maps north coast of Australia (New Holland)* |
| Roundheads lay siege to Colchester | 1648 | *Parliament tries Charles I for treason.* |
| | 1649 | *King Charles executed* |
| Samuel Pepys visits Audley End | 1659 | *Richard Cromwell resigns* |
| | 1660 | *Charles II returns from exile* |
| Richard Haddock commands 'Royal James' | 1672 | *Battle of Southwold Bay: 3rd Anglo-Dutch Naval War until 1674* |
| Samuel Pepys elected as MP for Harwich | 1685 | *Judge Jeffreys holds Bloody Assizes* |
| Daniel Defoe opens Brickworks | 1694 | *Bank of England is founded* |
| Daniel Defoe jailed for sedition | 1703 | *Death of Samuel Pepys* |
| Death of Sir Richard Haddock | 1715 | *Jaccobite revolt put down* |
| Birth of Dick Turpin | 1705 | *Construction of Blenheim Palace* |
| Walton Tower Built | 1721 | *Robert Walpole becomes the first prime minister of Britain* |
| Fairlop Fair begins in earnest | 1725 | *Black Watch founded in Scotland* |
| First recorded race at Galleywood | 1770 | *Birth of Poet William Wordsworth* |
| Tide Mill contructed at Battlesbridge | 1775 | *American Revolution begins* |
| Crown acquires Gunpowder Factory at Waltham Abbey | 1775 | *James Watt's builds prototype steam engine* |
| Essex & Kent 'Cricket' Match Tilbury | 1776 | *Declaration of Independence USA* |
| Richard Rigby investigated | 1781 | *First Building Society, in Birmingham.* |
| Lifeboat models first tested in Great Dunmow | 1784 | *Benjamin Franklin invents bifocals* |
| John Constable leaves Dedham school | 1793 | *Louis XVI of France executed* |
| Chelmer Navigation fully opened | 1797 | *Nore and Spithead Naval mutinies* |
| Sir Eliab Harvey takes command of the Essex Sea Fencibles | 1798 | *Irish Insurrection defeated* |

# CANVEY DUTCH COTTAGE

*Wooden clogs wait on the fender*
*As though their owner still lived here.*
*A tribute to Vermmuyden's skilful past*
*Designed by this Dutchman – built to last.*

The Canvey Dutch Cottage Museum on Canvey Road has been renovated by Castle Point Council as a monument to Dutch influences on the island's early development. Probably built in 1618 by Dutchman Julius Sludder, it was a teashop during the 1950s. Previously it had been home to a family of eight. It is one of two surviving cottages. The other, dated 1621, is still a private house.

Their design was unique for the time. Most English dwellings of that size would almost certainly be built of wood, whereas these cottages were built with brick, small industrial type bricks unknown in England at that time and probably imported from Holland. Their octagonal shape was unusual. In one of the cottages a number of cartwheels were discovered embedded in the earth floor, arranged around, and all touching a central wheel. This formation has been found in the Netherlands in the base of some types of wind and water mills as well as in some Flemish horse mills.

The cottages were built just before the first serious attempt at land reclamation and protection from the encroaching sea. In the early seventeenth century the principal landowners on the island were Sir Henry Appleton and Abigail Baker, however secondary but sizeable lands were also owned by John, William and Mary Blackmore, Thomas Bincker and Julius Sludder mentioned above. In 1623 Sir Henry Appleton proposed a project to reclaim land from the sea, which would protect their existing land and expand their holdings. The project would be financed by Appleton's associate, Joas Croppenburg, a wealthy London merchant. In return Croppenburg would take ownership of one third of all the reclaimed land. This share was to become known as the 'Third Acre Lands'.

Joas Croppenburg was related to Cornelius Vermuyden, a young Dutch engineer who was acquiring a growing reputation. Vermuyden was in England to oversee the restoration of a breach in the sea wall at Dagenham. He had also been responsible for projects of drainage and land reclamation in the East Anglian Fens.

Engaged to organise the Canvey project, Vermuyden brought three hundred workmen from Holland to build the new sea walls and drain the reclaimed land. His skill and the success of the project were recognised when, knighted by King Charles I, he became Sir Cornelius Vermuyden. He is remembered and commemorated to this day by the Canvey School that bears his name.

Many of the Dutch workers were paid with grants of 'Third Acre' land and settled with their families. They had much work to do before they could reap the benefits of farming their land. The cost of maintaining the sea walls, though high, was one they bore willingly to protect their investment in their new lives. Some of the English so-called 'Freeland' owners however were not quite so meticulous in keeping to their obligations which resulted in flooding which disheartened their neighbours. Over time some Dutchmen sold up, and moved away. Those that stayed formed the nucleus of a strong, and lasting, Dutch influence on the island.

By the late eighteenth century the sea walls had again deteriorated. A season of fierce tides breached the walls causing severe damage in 1791. The following year Parliament was petitioned with an act for "effectively embanking, draining and otherwise improving the Island of Canvey in the County of Essex". Since then the sea defences have been more or less continually upgraded. They were of course seriously overwhelmed in the floods of 1953 (see page 172, the Great Surge). However Vermuyden's work had not all been in vain.

Canvey Island had about 500 residents at the beginning of the twentieth century and only grew significantly when the first permanent road bridge to South Benfleet was opened in 1931. The Dutch had shown the way forward and the community that exists today may not have been possible without them.

# BILLERICAY PIONEERS

*They abandoned their roots for a New World life,*
*Fleeing persecution and intolerance which under*
*King James' rule was rife.*

The 'Mayflower', under its master Christopher Jones from Harwich, set sail from Plymouth on the 6th September 1620. They were headed for the 'New World' across the Atlantic Ocean. With a crew of 35 the Mayflower carried 102 pioneers, now known as the 'Pilgrim Fathers'. One of them died on the voyage and one new 'Pilgrim' was born. Landfall at Cape Cod, in present-day Massachusetts, was achieved 66 days later after an arduous 2,750 nautical mile journey.

Amongst the group were four from Billericay, Essex: Christopher Martin, his wife Marie, step-son Solomon Prower and their servant John Langmore. They became known as the Billericay Pioneers. Within three months of making landfall half of the Pilgrims died in the harsh winter conditions, including all those from Billericay. Nevertheless the new colony survived. More Pilgrims arrived on ships that sailed from Essex in the following years and one of the foundations of the new American nation was laid.

The Pilgrims differed from other colonists. They were not going to the New World to seek their fortune but to escape religious persecution. In order to get to the New World they were financed by enterprising groups known as Merchant Adventurers. The sole aim of these groups was commercial profit. Some of them viewed the 'Pilgrims' as expendable colonists but a useful form of labour.

Christopher Martin was an enigma. He ran a victualling, or wholesale food, business and may have been a miller too. There is evidence that he owned properties in the Billericay area. By all accounts he was difficult to deal with. He had had several clashes with fellow traders, local authorities, the local church and even fellow worshippers. Perhaps he thought that by joining the 'Pilgrims' he could further his business aims. Maybe he just wanted to get away from people he didn't get on with.

Somehow, before the ship had sailed, Martin became treasurer with responsibility for organising provisions for the 'Pilgrims' voyage. Then surprisingly, he was elected Governor of the first colony.

It didn't take long for Martin to fall out with almost everyone he had dealings with. The Merchant Adventurers were constantly irritated by his uncoordinated way of acquiring stores. His haughty attitude and refusal to supply accounts for what he purchased aggrieved his fellow 'Pilgrims'.

Things came to a head before the Mayflower was due to sail when his fellow 'Pilgrims' overwhelmingly passed a vote of no confidence and replaced him as governor.

Christopher Martin still chose to go on the Mayflower. It may be that he had committed so much capital on matters connected with the voyage and had nothing to return to in Essex.

The 'Pilgrims' were not the first group from England to cross the Atlantic. In 1585, with Sir Walter Raleigh, 100 settlers arrived at Roanoke Island, Chesapeake Bay in present day Virginia. Two years later all trace of them had gone. Roanoke had become the lost colony. In 1607 another settlement was founded in the same area at Jamestown. Despite the relatively benign environment it also almost didn't survive. Another Harwich man, Christopher Newport, captained the small flotilla that took these colonists to Jamestown.

Essex has left its mark on Massachusetts today. Within the state there is not only an Essex County and the town of Essex, there is also a Chelmsford, a Braintree, a Harwich and of course a Billerica although it mysteriously lost its 'y' whilst crossing the Atlantic.

The *Merchant Adventurers* who financed and organised the expeditions to America, under the patronage of the crown, also allocated the land. Originally the parcels of land marked out were called **Hundreds** although they became more commonly known as plantations.

# Say 'I Do, Pay the Fee, Sign the book'

*The false name she gave was the one he took;*
*'Just pay the fee, say 'I do' and sign the book.'*

It is often said that trouble comes in threes. Gilbert Dillingham, Brian Walton and Samuel Smith succeeded each other as Rectors of St Andrews Church, Sandon near Chelmsford, and proved the rule rather than the exception.

Just over 400 years ago, in 1601, Gilbert Dillingham took up his position and moved into the rectory. The reign of Queen Elizabeth was drawing to a close and the new monarch would be James I. For the first time in the history of the British Isles the crowns of England and Scotland would be united.

For Dillingham, like all past Rectors at Sandon, the office held many benefits. Comfortable lodgings were provided together with a reasonable income from the *tithe.* This was a 10% tax levied on the profits from land and stock falling within the parish. Gifts from wealthy benefactors were also added to the church coffers as well as the plate collections and fees from weddings, christening and funeral services. Furthermore in the early 1600s church attendance was compulsory for all parishioners.

On the surface Gilbert Dillingham appeared quite content with his lot and for 14 years nothing much changed. However the Rector was working on a scheme to boost his income from weddings. Prior to 1615, St Andrews Church hosted an average of four weddings a year. Word spread quickly of the Rector's new scheme and suddenly, almost overnight, Sandon was the place to go to be married quickly. With *'Instant Weddings'* on offer, lovesick grooms and would be brides were heading for Sandon from far and wide.

Few questions were asked and little if anything was done to verify the answers given. In many cases false names were used and many 'Mr and Mrs Smiths' departed happily after the ceremony. Gilbert Dillingham's biggest coup was to marry off the daughter of a neighbouring vicar. There was only one condition - the wedding fee was to be promptly paid on the day.

During his tenure the Reverent Dillingham conducted over 500 weddings. So while Gretna Green* or even Las Vegas spring to mind as places for couples looking for a quick way to tie the knot it was Sandon in Essex that pioneered the quickie wedding. In 1636 Gilbert Dillingham retired and was never heard of again.

Brian Walton, the next Rector, was a biblical scholar. He took his duties very seriously and was baffled when couples who had no connection with the parish began turning up hoping for a speedy wedding. Walton, who wanted to move on to greater things in the church hierarchy, immediately put a stop to the wedding business much to the consternation of his would be customers. The new Rector did not hold his post for long though. In 1641 the dark clouds of the English Civil war were looming and Walton, as a committed Royalist was 'removed'. He fled to staunchly royalist Oxford shortly afterwards.

The next Rector appointed at Sandon was Samuel Smith. Contemporary records describe him as a *very low churchman*. He had a puritanical outlook much in tune with the ascendant Cromwellian values of the day. Smith was rector for nearly 20 years. In that time he managed to upset many of the congregation and was enthusiastic in summoning them for non-attendance.

Although the previous rector, Brian Walton, was supposedly on the run, he still tried to get his hands on the *tithe* income from Sandon. It is difficult to imagine, bearing in mind the primitive communications of the time, how he could achieve his objective. Walton's efforts sufficiently annoyed Samuel Smith to prompt him to write a letter of complaint to a Parliamentary committee. The committee, being no friend of Royalist sympathisers, immediately issued a warrant for Walton's arrest.

More drama was to follow at the Sandon Rectory. In 1660, following the death of Oliver Cromwell, the monarchy was restored. Now Samuel Smith was out of favour. Orders were given to 'remove' him. However Smith decided he would have none of it and barricaded himself in. All attempts at persuasion to leave were rejected and eventually the bailiffs were called. They broke in through the rectory roof and dragged him out.

Theoretically Brian Walton was restored as Rector but a greater calling came. He took up the post of chaplain to King Charles II and was then elevated to Bishop of Chester. As for Sandon rectory the last of the troublesome occupants had gone. William Wells became rector and church affairs have remained calm ever since.

* Gretna Green did not become a 'Wedding destination' until 1754.

# LEIGH FISHY TALES.

*Legends abound of smuggled brandy and tea*
*And Leigh men have always lived from the sea*
*Some became Admirals and were highly revered*
*While some were 'pressed' many more volunteered.*

The raised brick tomb of Mary Ellis with its flat altar stone topping, standing just outside the entrance porch of St Clement's Church, bears the epitaph, *"Here lies the body of Mary Ellis, daughter of Thomas & Lydia Ellis of this parish. She was a virgin of virtuous courage & promising hope and died on the 3rd of June 1609 aged 119"*.

Amusing as this is, the strange markings on top of the altar stone tell a less amusing story. The seventeenth century was the beginning of the age of the dreaded naval press gangs. The Navy was desperately short of men and places like Leigh-on-Sea, with a strong fishing tradition, were prime recruiting grounds. When unable to meet their quotas elsewhere the press gangs, on Sundays, would sometimes wait in St Clement's churchyard for men to emerge from the service. They would stand around Mary Ellis's tomb and while waiting sharpen their cutlasses on its top, thus giving it its nickname of 'The Cutlass Stone'. Fortunately for the young men of Leigh the noise of sharpening could be heard in the church, warning those of the age to be threatened. They quickly disappeared down a hidden underground tunnel to the cellar of the Rectory where they would await the all clear from the Sexton. The press gangs would watch disappointedly as the congregation emerged, consisting only of women, children and old men well passed naval service.

How much of this story is true and how much legend is a matter of conjecture. What cannot be inferred from it is that the men of Leigh were averse to serving their country.

History is littered with the names of Leigh men who rose to fame by doing their duty. The Haddock family, residents of Leigh for four hundred years, came to fame in the seventeenth century when William Haddock became Commander of *'The America'* fighting against the Dutch in 1653.

Perhaps the most famous Haddock was Richard, also a captain in the Navy. He commanded *'The Royal James'* and was wounded at the battle of Sole Bay in 1672. Subsequently promoted to Admiral and Comptroller of the Navy, he also represented Aldeburgh in parliament in 1678. He became MP for Shoreham in 1685-7, as well as being Master of Trinity House. His eldest son, another Richard, was also to become Comptroller of the Navy. Nicholas, his younger son, was created Admiral of the Blue in 1744.

The Salmon family lived in Leigh for three hundred years and between 1588 and 1641 three generations, all named Robert, were Masters of Trinity House.

Another Leigh family, the Goodlads, were shipbuilders to Queen Elizabeth the first. William Goodlad, who commanded the Greenland Fleet for twenty years, was also Master of Trinity House when he died in 1638. There seems to have been something of a tradition of Leigh men becoming Masters of Trinity House. Richard Chester, who lived on Strand Wharf, was appointed to the role in 1615.

Much later William Brand from Leigh commanded *'The Revenge'* and fought with Nelson at Trafalgar. For centuries Leigh men have played a part in our seafaring traditions, right up to modern times when the *'Little Ships of Leigh'* sailed to Dunkirk. (see page 160)

Of course there are other aspects to the endeavours of Leigh's men of the sea. Ever since excise duties were introduced smuggling has been practised. Leigh, with its shallow tidal creeks and marshes, was a smugglers' haven. The Customhouse in Leigh was built on Strand Wharf in 1738, although the first customs officer was appointed in 1565. Since then and into the nineteenth century Leigh fishermen have played hide and seek with the excise men. Some of today's well-known families such as the Cotgroves and the Dowsetts could claim ancestors that made a good living from smuggling.

One of the more successful was George Walter whose father Edward Newton Walter was Rector of St Clement's Church. George, a retired Marine Officer, organised the local sailors so that their operations were like military manoeuvres. His father the Rector and other dignitaries were always looked after with a token share of the contraband.

Rumours persist to this day of secret tunnels built to evade the customs. One of these was proven when in 1892 fire broke out in 'The Peterboat' tavern. It was burnt to the ground exposing a secret cellar beneath the main cellar, with direct access to the waterfront, where contraband goods were stored.

The remains of the houses next to the pub showed evidence of trapdoors to interconnecting attics between houses. This meant that goods could be dispersed and hidden before being loaded onto carts and taken up to the no-mans-land of Daws Heath. There they would be distributed to dealers and middlemen for onward transport to London and beyond. The contraband included not only the ever popular brandy, sherry, tea, coffee and tobacco but also silks, brocades, Flemish lace, leather goods and jewellery. In fact anything that was in demand and carried a high duty.

The rewards were high but the penalties if caught were equally severe. At times the smugglers were offered an amnesty in return for volunteering to serve three years in the Navy. Unsurprisingly there is little evidence of this happening on any scale in Leigh.

# WITNESSES IN WHITE

*With elegant long necks and stately progress*
*The swans in numbers glide,*
*From Manningtree to Mistley*
*Along the river Stour both clear and wide.*

For centuries, probably, swans have been gliding gracefully on the River Stour between Mistley and Manningtree. Back in the seventeenth century however this north east corner of Essex was a hotbed of Puritan support for Oliver Cromwell's Roundheads in the raging English civil war. It was against this background that Matthew Hopkins set himself up as Witch-Finder General. In 1645 he began a campaign of terror, mostly against poor and vulnerable women.

Much of what is known of Hopkins is speculative. No known records exist of his birth and early years, his education or training. He was probably born in Mistley around 1619. The only record of his death is a note in a book published in 1854 stating: *In an ancient parish register belonging to the parish of Midley-cun-Manningtree, commencing in 1559 is the following entry: "Matthew Hopkins, son of Mr James Hopkins, Minister of Wenham, was buried at Mistley, August 12th, 1647."*

He was a much-feared informer known to the authorities as 'compliant'. He was assisted in his fourteen-month reign of terror by fellow 'Witch-Pricker'\* John Sterne. Together they were responsible for the condemnation and execution of more than 200 alleged witches.

Hopkins began locally, accusing Elizabeth Clarke, a poor one-legged woman whose mother had been hanged as a witch and had her committed to prison. He personally interrogated her with Sterne's help and used torture, though it was illegal, to obtain a confession that incriminated five other women. The investigation spread to over a hundred people being interrogated, gaining more confessions. Eventually thirty-two women were tried at a special court in Chelmsford in July 1645. Of these twenty-nine were condemned to be hanged, ten of them at Chelmsford. Four according to Hopkins, at Mistley, *"to be hanged at where their Discoverer lives, this for sending the Devil like a Bear to kill him."* The rest were hanged at various villages throughout the county.

These were troublesome times and thankfully the witch hysteria died down to a great extent after the sixteen-forties.

Local legend has it that Hopkins' ghost haunts Mistley Pond and a figure in seventeenth century clothing is seen on Friday nights at the time of the Witches Sabbats\*. The visitor standing on the banks of the Stour watching the swans, however will be blissfully unaware of this.

\*Witch-pricker, the assistant who would search an alleged witch for marks of the Devil. Witches Sabbats: There are 8 sabbats, 4 major, May Eve, Midsummer Day, Lammas (1st August) and Halloween and 4 lesser, Yule (usually Christmas day), Candlemas (approximately 2 February), Spring Equinox and Fall Equinox.

# Under Siege

*On the ninth of June they invaded the town*
*Things in their way just got knocked down.*
*Lucas and Lisle had the Royalist command,*
*Townspeople in fear of the army's demands.*

In 1648 the people of Colchester, in common with most of the population, were fed up with years of war. The King, Charles I, had given himself up to Cromwell's Parliamentarians. It must have seemed as if a deal would soon be done and peace would reign once again.

There were, however, significant pockets of Royalist supporters with other ideas. One of these was an army of some 3,000 men led by George Goring, the Earl of Norwich. Defeated at Maidstone, they had fled across the Thames to seek loyalist reinforcements in Essex. Heading north, hotly pursued by Lord Fairfax's Roundheads, they joined with Sir George Lisle and a force from Hertfordshire.

On reaching Colchester the Cavaliers, now numbering more than 5,500, decided to make a stand and fight. The Burghers of Colchester, terrified of occupation, barred the gates and posted sixty guards to prevent access. Sir Charles Lucas, a Royalist commander who came from Colchester, charged the gates. The guards fled and on the 9th of June the town was occupied. Colchester now had five and a half thousand extra mouths to feed from resources already much depleted by years of Civil War.

The Parliamentary forces, under General Lord Fairfax, arrived on the 12th of June. Inside the gates the Earl of Norwich then announced to the townspeople that he would, *take them into His Majesty's protection and fight the enemy in that situation.*

The citizens were trapped within the walls in exactly the situation the Burghers had feared. For eleven weeks Colchester was under siege. The Parliamentarians encircled the town, digging trenches and earthworks. By July 1st the town was effectively cut off and the siege began to bite. Persistent efforts by Royalist troops to break out were beaten back. No one military or civilian was allowed out, the siege was complete.

Whatever food there was the army requisitioned, as well as forcibly recruiting townsmen and their weapons. By mid July horses were being slaughtered for food. In August people were reduced to eating cats, dogs, and even rats. With starvation at hand and no prospect of relief, on the 27th of August, the Royalists surrendered.

When the victors entered the town they were shocked at the sorry state of both the town and the inhabitants. Cruelly there was no sympathy for the people; instead they were fined heavily for allowing the King's men into their town in the first place.

Two Royalist commanders, Sir Charles Lucas and Sir George Lisle, were tried and summarily executed by firing squad. Their leader, the Earl of Norwich, escaped with his life, being of the aristocracy his fate was left for Parliament to decide. Many of the surviving rank and file soldiers were savagely treated and subsequently deported to the West Indies to work as slave labour.

# Dear Diary
## Audley End

*To view Audley End House in its beautiful grounds,*
*The whole of the place could not be better found.*

Samuel Pepys had a varied and busy life. In 1649 he was present at the execution of Charles I. He lived through the Great Plague in London and, in 1666, The Great Fire. He was imprisoned twice and remarkably managed to become the Member of Parliament for Harwich. (See 'Elected by 32' next chapter)

However, Samuel Pepys is best remembered for his diary which he began in 1660 and kept for 10 years until failing eyesight forced him to lay down his pen. Pepys never intended the diaries for publication. They were personal and written in unusual shorthand. Twenty five years after his death the diaries were 'discovered'. Almost a century later in 1825 they were published. The diaries give a wealth of period detail that had not been available before in a written form.

An entry on Monday 27th February 1660 records Pepys' visit to Audley End near Saffron Walden with his friend Mr Blaydon. He described his visit to the house and gardens as '*exceedingly worth seeing*'. He paid particular attention to the '*stateliness of the ceilings, chimney-pieces*' and the portraits, especially, those of the *Four Evangelists* and *Henry VIII*. During the visit he was invited, or invited himself, down to the cellars with the housekeeper where upon, '*we drank most admirable drink and toasted the Kings health*'.

Pepys, being an accomplished musician and '*there being an excellent echo*' then entertained those present on his *flageolette*. Later, somewhat inebriated, he visited the local almshouse '*where forty poor people was maintained*'. More drink was consumed before adjourning to the local Inn where he proceeded to flirt with the '*daughter of the house, she being very pretty*'.

Henry VIII gave the estate to Lord Audley in 1535, after the dissolution of the Abbey, which stood on the site. Hence the name Audley End. Thomas Howard, 1st Earl of Suffolk, a descendant of Lord Audley built the present house in 1614. It was at the time the largest house in England. All the contents of the house were sold in 1745 following the death of the 10th Earl of Suffolk. The whereabouts of the paintings mentioned in the 'Diary' are unknown.

Over the years the house has been modified and changed many times. In the late 1770s Sir John Griffin Griffin* employed the architect Robert Adams and the landscape gardener Lancelot (Capability) Brown to renovate the house and gardens.

During World War II, the Special Operations Executive used the house as a base for training agents undertaking secret operations in occupied Poland. There is a memorial to the agents killed on active service in the gardens. After the war the Ministry of Works purchased the House for £30,000. The house and grounds are now managed by English Heritage.

Today, as a tribute to Samuel Pepys, two abridged volumes of the diaries are kept in the library.

*Yes his name really was Sir John Griffin Griffin*

**Audley End House**

# ELECTED BY 32

*Elections were not considered suitable at that stage,*
*As for public opinion, that was impossible to gauge.*

In the British general election of 2005, the parliamentary seat of Harwich and Clacton had an electorate of some 80,000. One Member of Parliament was elected to serve the constituency. There were six candidates.

Four hundred years ago when James I granted Harwich its Royal Charter, the adult (over 16) population was fewer than 800, living in approximately 150 dwellings. However on 5th February 1679, two Members of Parliament were elected to represent the town. The electoral role was precisely 32. As far as is known there were no other candidates contesting the vacant seats. Harwich was considered a truly '*rotten*' borough.

The two MPs chosen were the celebrated diarist Samuel Pepys who was working for the admiralty, and Sir Anthony Deane, a master shipwright. The electorate of 32 consisted of the serving members of Harwich town council. Council members held office until they were too old or ill to carry on or resigned. The only way they could be removed from office was if found guilty of misdemeanour by their colleagues. Earlier Christopher Jones, remembered as captain of the *Mayflower,* had been a councillor.

The fact that Harwich had two Parliamentarians raised eyebrows in some quarters. The town was a growing seaport with strategic defence and commercial interests. The harbour was a good source of revenue from customs dues and postal monies. In the eyes of some Government departments Harwich was an extremely important asset to have under their control. Accordingly every effort was made to ensure all municipal positions of importance were filled by departmental loyalists.

To begin with two Government departments, the Treasury and that of the Postmaster General, competed fiercely with each other to ensure council positions were given to their own men. Local agents were employed to smooth the way for their paymaster's respective nominations. They had few qualms, using bribes or blackmail to get their way. Later, as the navy grew in size, the War Office also competed for influence.

Religious intolerance stalked the land in 1679. A fevered atmosphere gripped the country when a catholic 'plot' to murder the King was unearthed. It was later found to be a complete hoax. Pepys, a supporter of the catholic Duke of York, found himself caught in the crossfire. He was jailed for 2 months in the Tower of London on charges of treachery. The charges were later dismissed.

In 1714 George I, the first of the Hanoverians* became King. The port of Harwich soon became the preferred gateway of travel for British Royals travelling back and forth from their native homeland in Germany.

Politics however had not changed, nor would they throughout the Hanoverian dynasty. The historian, Sir Lewis Bernstein Namier, published in 1929 a detailed exposé of the corruption and intrigue rife in Harwich in his book *The Structure of Politics at the Accession of George III*.

Things began to improve for Harwich after 1832 when the first great reform act was introduced. This established the principal of gaining office by popular vote as opposed to votes of the chosen few. Harwich was not the only 'rotten' borough. More that 50 others were abolished in a surge of widespread electoral reform. This new move to democracy met with considerable resistance from some existing office holders.

By 1835 Harwich council was on course to be elected by popular vote. Eligibility was extended to all male ratepayers owning property worth more than £10 a year in rent. Yet even in 1859 there were only 317 names on the Harwich and Dovercourt electoral role. Ten years later Harwich's Parliamentary representation was reduced to one.

Over the years Harwich has seen many changes to its electoral boundaries and there is more change in the pipeline. In the next general election Harwich will no longer be joined with Clacton. The constituency will be extended further west along the River Stour and it is assumed that all residents over the age of 18 will be able to exercise their right to vote.

*George I had become Elector of Hanover on the death of his mother the Electress Sophia. Two months later he became the first of the English Royal House of Hanover when he succeeded his cousin Queen Anne in 1714. Although 52nd in line to the throne he was the nearest protestant contender.

# THE BRICK MAKER OF CHADWELL ST MARY

*Daniel Defoe was doing well.*
*His factory made tiles and bricks to sell.*

Daniel Defoe, considered the founder of the English novel, is best remembered for penning *Robinson Crusoe*. He was 59 when the book was released and it was a literary sensation. Less well known perhaps is Defoe's political and business career, much of it surrounded in mystery and intrigue.

Defoe was probably born in Cripplegate, London, in 1660 or 1661, the son of James and Alice Foe – he was later to change his name to the grander sounding Defoe. However there has been speculation as to whether James and Alice were his real parents and that he may have been adopted. This stems from a tale that, on a late July evening, a newly born baby was brought from London to Chadwell's St Mary the Virgin church in Essex to be baptised as Daniel.

Whether Daniel was adopted or not his parents who were 'dissenters', were caring and gave him a good non-conformist home and education. The years surrounding Daniel's birth and formative years were turbulent. After the death of Oliver Cromwell, Charles II had been restored to the throne, religious intolerance stalked the land and plots to overthrow the monarchy were rife. A succession of Anglo – Dutch Wars broke out and London was hit by the great plague followed by the great fire.

From an early age Daniel Defoe had an entrepreneurial flair combined with an ability to borrow money to fund his schemes. In 1678, still under 20, he came to Tilbury and speculatively bought a long lease on a parcel of land. In London he diversified, establishing a hosiery business and involving himself in shipping, importing civet cats. He was also a prime mover in a diving bell venture to recover sunken treasure. A strong supporter of the 'dissenters' he was active in the 'political' movement that railed against the established church and was involved in the unsuccessful Monmouth rebellion of 1685 against King James II.

In November 1688 another momentous event convulsed England - 'The Glorious Revolution'. James II was effectively overthrown and replaced in a bloodless coup by William III from Holland.

Daniel Defoe welcomed this change. His writing and political activities had made him many friends in the new order. However his tangled business life was catching up with him. Many of Defoe's enterprises seem to have suffered ill fortune, or simply mismanagement, and numerous creditors were pursuing him. His personal life was equally complicated and costly as he maintained three 'wives' houses and was responsible for at least nine children. As well as his legal wife, Mary Tuffey, with whom he had seven children, he also maintained houses for 'private wife' Elizabeth Sammen in London and 'private wife' Mary Norton in Tilbury. His luck ran out though and in October 1692 he was jailed for bankruptcy with debts of £17,000.

In spite of this Defoe managed to bounce back. On release from prison he took up a prestigious post with the commissioners of the glass duty and also became a trustee of the royal lottery - both government jobs.

Although bankrupted, he had managed to hang on to his land in Tilbury. With income from his 'day' jobs and yet more borrowed money, he set up a brick factory in Chadwell St Mary specialising in the manufacture of roof tiles. Defoe had connections in the right places and acquired contracts to supply tiles for a number of prestigious projects such as the new Greenwich Hospital.

Things began to look up for Daniel Defoe, he lived in grand style. He had a large house close to Tilbury Fort plus a carriage, footmen and a pleasure boat. Yet he was continually distracted from brick making by his writing and politics. His efforts in getting published were bearing fruit. The public, and thus the book trade, had a growing appetite for 'expert' comment on politics, business, law and order and travel. Defoe was well placed to write authentically on these. However the brick factory was continually beset by problems. One of the biggest local employers, with at least 100 families on the payroll, it was grossly overstaffed. Defoe was inclined to employ anyone who asked for a job, whether suitably qualified or not.

The factory's products were considered shoddy and customers complained that the tiles were too porous. Defoe was so wrapped up in his political writings that the complaints were ignored. In 1703 he produced a satirical pamphlet, *The Shortest Way with Dissenters.* This caused fury in the establishment, the church and especially with the new monarch Queen Anne. Defoe was arrested, pilloried and convicted of sedition. Being imprisoned was the final straw and despite the best efforts of his brother-in-law the Brick Factory went under.

On his release from prison, with the act of Union between England and Scotland looming, Defoe was given a new challenge by one of his friends and patron Lord Harley - that of intelligence gathering. This was of course totally secretive as apart from anything else various factions within the Government continually plotted against each other. Daniel was the ideal candidate, as being a highly skilled writer, the dark arts of propaganda and spin came quite naturally. Yet Defoe had not given up his business ambitions and following the tremendous success of *Robinson Crusoe,* he purchased a lease on land at Mile End in Colchester with his daughter Hannah (by Mary Tuffey) once more with ambitions to build a brick factory, although this came to nothing.

Daniel Defoe may have been a hopeless brick maker but he was a talented and prolific writer. He was credited with publishing over 560 books and pamphlets and is considered by some to be the founder of British journalism. However he died alone, in debt and on the run from his creditors. Daniel Defoe junior acquired the land at Tilbury but disposed of it on the death of his father. Today all trace of the original factory has been erased.

Returning to Defoe's most famous novel, *Robinson Crusoe,* in the story Crusoe is befriended by 'Man Friday'. It just so happens that a neighbouring farmer on Daniel Defoe's Tilbury land was called John Friday. This information and much else about Daniel Defoe's Tilbury connection was unearthed, if that is the right word, by Thurrock historian Randal Bingley following an in depth study of 90 years worth of *'Court of Sewers Order Book, Oct 1646 - Feb 1735'* held in the Essex Records Office.

# STAND AND DELIVER

*"Stand and Deliver," these words of dread*
*Dick Turpin is reputed to have said.*

Somehow a myth grew up that has led to Dick Turpin being honoured in the names of dozens of pubs and eateries up and down the country. Further plaudits came through film, television, books and comics depicting him as a latter day Robin Hood who took from the rich and gave to the poor. The Dick Turpin character has also been embraced by some 'Heritage' sites where factual credence to the entirely fictional horse 'Black Bess' is given. Even more bizarrely he is acknowledged in dozens of journals and websites connected with the meat and sausage trade!

However the real Dick Turpin, born in Hempstead, north Essex in 1705, was totally devoid of glamour. He was hanged as a common criminal at Knavesmire, York at the age of 34.

Dick Turpin began employment as an apprentice butcher (hence the meat connection above) and then possibly ran a butchers shop in Thaxted. Allegedly he involved himself with stolen animals which ended his career in the meat business. Turpin then moved on to petty crime, graduating from deer rustling to smuggling. Around 1732 Turpin teamed up with Samuel Gregory in what was to become known as the *Gregory* or *Essex Gang*. Over a two year period a series of horrific robberies was committed in Essex and London. The gang had no compunction about torturing or beating their victims or violating any women found on the premises whilst the robbery was in progress.

Large rewards were offered for the capture of the gang and one by one the outlaws were apprehended. Turpin though managed to remain at large but with a considerable price on his head. He went to ground, surfacing again in 1737 to team up with another villain known as Matthew (or Tom) King. More robberies followed which often resulted in cold blooded murder. However the net was closing and King was tracked to Whitechapel in east London. Turpin rode to the rescue but all he achieved was to shoot his accomplice in the melee. On his death bed Tom King confessed all. Meanwhile Dick Turpin fled north and assumed the name John Palmer. In spite of this time was running out. 'Palmer' was arrested on an unrelated matter and put in York jail. Letters he penned to relatives identified the prisoner as the real Dick Turpin.

Convicted on two indictments, Turpin was sentenced to death. On 7th April, 1739, Dick Turpin was put on an open cart and taken through the streets of York watched by gawping crowds. He met his end on the scaffold at York racecourse.

*Nearly 100 years later a legend was created through the popular 1834 novel 'Rookwood' written by Harrison Ainsworth. The horse 'Black Bess' was a fictional creation of the writer and all the rest is just - let us say 'history'.*

# WALTON TOWER

*Through the mist we see you now*
*A column of unchanging certainty*
*Walton Tower blesses us in our sights*
*As we sail hard across the sea.*

Walton Tower is 80 feet high and sits on top of the 70 feet Naze cliffs. Built by Trinity House it was a navigational marker for ships approaching the port of Harwich. That was in 1721 and today it is still a comforting sight to East Coast sailors coming back to shore. Sadly future generations may not benefit from this prominent landmark.

The Naze, from which Walton takes its name, is an area of headland known the world over for its ancient fossils and unique wildlife. In common with much of the East Coast however it fights an ongoing, and losing, battle against the sea. The Tower currently stands some 50 feet from the cliff edge. It has been calculated that within twenty years it will be demolished, unless action is taken to stem the alarming rate of erosion of the cliffs.

Past events give some idea of the sea's relentless power. The old Parish Church of All Saints, belonging to the Diocesan estate of London's St Paul's Cathedral, was washed away completely in 1796. This victim of coastal erosion is now called *'Prebenda Consumpta per Mare'* (The church eaten by the sea). The waves have now advanced several hundred feet beyond the place where the church once stood. Local legend has it that stormy seas caused coffins to float ashore and that people made good use of the timber. There are even tales of sunken church bells being heard.

Originally farmland, the Naze became a private golf course. During the Second World War it was requisitioned by the ministry of defence as a lookout location and in 1967 the local council purchased the area as a public open space. Since then it has been enjoyed by thousands of visitors and residents every year.

In 1998 the Tower, unique of its kind and in a dilapidated condition, was bought by local businessman Edward Charman with a dream of restoring it to its former glory. His plan has been realised and the Tower is now a museum, art gallery and café.* During the summer months it is open daily to visitors. For a small fee one can learn of its history as well as gaining stunning views for miles around from the observation platform at the very top.

The Walton Backwaters, seen clearly from the top of the tower, are beloved of generations of small boat enthusiasts. They also provided Arthur Ransome with the inspiration for his famous children's adventure story *Swallows and Amazons*.

---

*There are precedents for a café in the tower. In 1770s the Naze tea rooms, opened by Richard Rigby, were the subject of a major scandal. (see page 78, Rigby's Follies)*

# THE FAIRLOP FRIGATE

*Daniel Day was accident prone, road travel made him quiver*
*A keen sailor, he was much more at home on the river.*

Two hundred years ago Hainault forest covered much of present day Ilford, Barkingside and Chigwell. It was also the home of the original Fairlop Oak. One of the largest trees ever seen in Britain, it is thought to have been given that name by Queen Anne on a visit in 1704. It grew on a spot occupied by the present day boathouse at Fairlop Water.

This enormous oak tree stood alone in a vast clearing and was the setting for the Fairlop Fair, which began in earnest in 1725. It became an annual event taking place during the first week in July and ran almost continuously until 1900. Its founder was the jovially eccentric Daniel Day.

Daniel Day was a wealthy man who had earned his fortune in marine engineering. He lived on the river Thames at Wapping. He also owned some cottages near Fairlop and made it his business to collect the rents there annually, usually on the first Friday in July. He decided to make this day a special occasion for his friends, his employees and his tenants. Bacon and beans were ordered from a local hostelry and a grand 'beanfeast' was held under the great canopy of the Fairlop Oak.

Within a few years others joined in and gradually the gathering turned into a gigantic fair. There would be puppeteers, circus acrobats and exotic animals on hand to provide entertainment. A market sprang up too, selling sweets, toys and nick knacks. To begin with the fair was described "*as most respected and well regulated*". In 1736 however the first prosecutions were recorded of stallholders for indulging in gaming and illegal liquor sales.

Day was nervous of travelling by road. He had been involved in a serious accident when his coach overturned. Accordingly he got his workers to put wheels on a masted boat which was decked out with rigging, flags and bunting. He would travel in style by river as far as possible and then by road for the beanfeast. On land the boat, nicknamed the Fairlop Frigate, was hauled by a team of six horses and preceded by a marching band.

In the 1750's 100,000 people came to the fair from all over London and the unregulated large crowds caused all sorts of problems. The fair also attracted pickpockets, conmen and opportunist thieves. In 1765 the local constabulary reported that, "*a great number of people meet in a riotous and tumultuous manner selling ale and spirituous liquors and keeping tippling booths and gaming tables to the great encouragement of vice and immorality*". In 1793 the Fair was banned but was revived the following year.

Daniel Day died in 1767 aged 84 and was buried a coffin fashioned from a branch that had fallen from the Fairlop Oak. He was buried in St. Margaret's Church yard, Barking. He had originally asked to be buried under the Fairlop Oak but his request was declined.

The Fairlop Oak suffered numerous acts of vandalism, particularly from fires lit inside its trunk by careless picnickers. Gradually the tree died and in 1820 it was blown down by a gale. The Fairlop Oak was no more. The fair however continued to grow, vying with the Derby on Epsom Downs as a semi-official holiday.

1839 saw one of the biggest crowds ever. 200,000 attended the fair. It was one of the biggest carnivals in London and the roads to the area were jammed. However not everyone approved. The Lord's Day Observance society frowned upon the proceedings as did the Religious Tract Society, a Christian book publisher, who counted 108 drinking booths and 72 gaming tables.

There was also increasing commercial pressure from developers and interested landowners to exclude the public from the forest. Despite a huge public protest an Act of Parliament was passed in 1851 that authorised the destruction of 3,000 acres of forest. Within six weeks over 10,000 trees were dug up using the most advanced steam engines of the day. It was state sponsored vandalism on an unprecedented scale that provoked local outrage. Much of the timber was sold off at bargain prices and there was widespread theft with a great deal of waste left to rot. Enclosed farmland then replaced the original forest with all public access barred.

The Fairlop Fair continued on alternative sites for another fifty years but declined gradually and ceased altogether in 1900.

Over the years several Fairlop Frigates were built. One built in 1812 was discovered in a Romford back garden in 1951; the hull was rotten, the wheels missing and the rigging and mast all gone. Today at Fullwell Cross, in the London Borough of Redbridge, there is a public house named *New Fairlop Oak*. In the same year as the frigate was found in Romford another oak tree was planted in the centre of the large roundabout facing the pub.

# THE QUEENS PLATE

*Stock Road was shut, hotels and inns full.*
*Schools closed as race day exerted its pull.*

On the green just outside Galleywood's Library stands the town sign depicting two jockeys racing. The background shows trees and the top of a church steeple further back. White fencing posts mark the edge of a racetrack. Also visible is what seems to be a VIP grandstand.

Horse racing ended at Galleywood in 1935. All that may be seen today of these images are St Michael's church and a few remaining white fencing posts along the side of Stock Road.

For 100 years Galleywood was one of the premier racecourses in the land. 1770 brought royal patronage when King George III promised to pay 100 guineas to the winner of a race. His Queen, Charlotte, offered a silver plate – hence the term The Queen's Plate.

Race meetings at Galleywood were extremely popular events and thousands of people travelled for miles for the occasion. The course was one of the longest in the country. It circled the village church and for the horses it had a killing uphill finish. When flat racing was replaced by steeple chasing the course developed a notable tag line:-

*Galleywood: Steeple chasing round a real steeple.*

With race days came all the fun of the fair. Apart from betting, there were entertainers of all shapes and sizes, prize fighting, cock and dog fighting. There was plenty of casual work on the track. In many instances farm labourers just abandoned their daily toil for the more exciting and relatively well paid work on the track, much to the chagrin of the local farmers.

The hotels and inns did a roaring trade and were packed solid. The police were kept busy too as the meetings attracted the usual array of pickpockets and con-men. The coming of the races was also eagerly looked forward to by local children. Schools were closed as a safely precaution because of the sheer numbers of people in the area and the amount of unfamiliar traffic.

In 1862 'The Chelmsford Race Company' was formed. It aimed to run the race meetings in a more organised fashion. The company proposed to build a grandstand and associated accommodation with strict rules as to who could be admitted to the stand. Usually the races were over two days. Horse racing attracted people from every social class, from the gentry to what were deemed the lower orders. Accordingly the first day was reserved for the gentry and their ladies. The second day was thrown open to the farmers, their workers and the townsfolk of Chelmsford. The fortunes of the racecourse fluctuated over the years, but the First World War brought a rapid decline.

The company ceased trading in 1922 and after that horse racing in Galleywood never recovered. In the economic depression that followed there were fewer and fewer spectators. Steeple chasing ended in 1935 and limited pony racing returned until the outbreak of war in 1939. After the Second World War much of the land was bought by Chelmsford council for housing. However the splendid open space of Galleywood common remains for all to enjoy.

# THREE MILLS AT BATTLESBRIDGE

*Here, the confluence of centuries –*
*Three mills-*
*Three histories of quern and staple –*
*Ground from their meaning by the tides of traffic.*

Two hundred years ago Battlesbridge was a self contained community with a busy harbour that acted as a logistics centre for Wickford, Rayleigh and most of the villages in the surrounding area. Coal, building materials, the new industrial goods made in London and even newspapers would be brought up the river Crouch for distribution. Vessels would then return loaded with flour, animal feed and agricultural produce from the farms nearby, all of which were needed to fuel London's ever expanding growth.

Battlesbridge was a milling town. The first mill constructed was a tide mill on the south side of the Crouch upstream from the bridge. Unfortunately the tide was an unreliable source of power and the venture was not deemed a success. In 1815, in the middle of celebrations commemorating the defeat of Napoleon at Waterloo, disaster struck when a careless worker entered the mill floor carrying a lighted candle. The building caught fire and the blaze severely damaged all the machinery.

The mill struggled on for another 20 years under a succession of owners, the last ending in bankruptcy. No effort was spared in advertising the business and a press notice of the day described the mill as having *'power almost unlimited'*.

The mill fell into disuse and the derelict site was acquired by William Meeson from Grays. Meeson owned quarries and several Thames Barges, the new backbone of transport around south eastern England. He immediately realised the mill's location upstream from the bridge was unsuitable as it restricted waterborne access.

A new mill was built on the north bank of the river east of the bridge. This one would be steam driven and it was completed in 1896. This is the building we see today called 'The Old Granary'. Its many floors now house an Antiques Centre. During the First World War another mill was built on the opposite, south, bank. Milling was obviously good business. William Meeson died in 1926 and the enterprise was taken over by J & G Matthews.

Fire disaster struck again and the mill on the south bank was completely destroyed. At the time of the fire the tide was out so there was no means of extinguishing the flames. Fire was a real hazard with mills and for a time Battlesbridge had its own fire station.

The Mill on the South Bank was rebuilt in 1933 but times were changing. The days of the Thames Barges were over as being a primary means of transport and Battlesbridge had lost its strategic importance as a distribution centre.

In 1960 the mills were acquired by British Oils and Cake Mills (BOCM) who made animal feeds. Trade continued to decline and both mills were closed within 5 years. During their time the mills had used water, steam, oil and electricity to power them.

The First World War mill on the south bank has since been partially demolished and the lower floors that remain are used for storage.

In 1967 Battlesbridge Antiques Centre took over the mill on the north bank. The Centre is now spread around five period buildings housing over 80 dealers and is the largest Antique Centre in Essex.

A common thread that connects the three mills at Battlesbridge, apart from their location on the river Crouch, was the regularity which they were damaged by fire or completely burnt down. The old tide mill buildings were destroyed again by fire in 1902 and for 80 years all that remained was the wheel channel and the tidal dam retaining wall. However the Hart family restored the mill and wheel in 1988. Although no milling is carried out, from the outside it looks much as it did its heyday.

# It's Not Cricket!

*One guard was bayoneted and the sergeant shot dead*
*Before Kent took to their boats and the Essex men fled.*

No one is sure precisely when cricket began, but it was sometime in the 1700s. It is often thought of as a genteel game of jolly good sportsmen where just to play is considered the most important aspect. Today's money driven agenda seems a far cry from that. Many also think of violence in sport as a late 20th century phenomenon, but judging by what happened nearly 250 years ago that view is somewhat misplaced!

The year was 1776. In Britain mad King George III was on the throne and America had just made its declaration of independence. In October, Essex were about to play Kent at cricket. County names were picked for teams at almost any level as it gave the match an element of prestige. In any event there was no county structure for cricket at that time. The substance of the story that follows is from a Gravesend letter published in the *London Chronicle* on 31st October 1776.

*The Essex and Kent teams had assembled on a pitch at Tilbury Fort. Following the usual pre-match competitive banter, for some reason the Essex team took exception to one of the Kent players and refused to play. This resulted in mayhem. One of the Kent men ran to the guard room and seized a weapon. Upon returning, in the ensuing fracas, the weapon was discharged and a man from the Essex side was shot dead. Immediately the remaining players stormed the guard room. One of the guards was run through with a bayonet and a sergeant, who intervened to try and calm the situation was also killed. Even more appalling was the fact that most of the personnel at the fort were disabled serviceman put on light duties. The Essex men eventually slunk away and the Kent men took to their boats and rowed back across the River Thames to Kent.*

This account remained unchallenged for 200 years when its authenticity was questioned by cricket buff Leslie Thomspon. He surmised that cricket would not have taken place at Tilbury in the first place or as late as October. What may be in his favour is that there are no records of any follow up by the law or further press reports of such a sensational incident.

On a lighter note, Essex County Cricket Club was not formed for another 100 years, in 1876 at Brentwood. It moved to the present Chelmsford ground in 1966. One hundred and three years later, in 1979, Essex won their first major trophies - the County Championship and the Benson & Hedges Cup. Happily there have been no repeats of the match of 1776.

**Settling the Score**

# RIGBY'S FOLLIES

*Beside the Stour two towers stand,*
*Relics of a scheme to make Mistley grand.*

In 1703 Aubrey de Vere, the 20th Earl of Oxford, died. His estates were divided between four of his aunts. Six years later a very surprised Edward Rigby, a linen draper in London, learned that he had inherited the village of Mistley and much of the surrounding countryside.

Mistley's two towers and the Swan Fountain, further to the east on the River Stour, are all that remain of a grand scheme to turn Mistley into a spa town. The idea was conceived by Richard Rigby, the grandson of Edward. One of the leading architects of the day Robert Adams, who was also involved in Audley End House, drew up the plans. Work began on the project in 1776.

Rigby owned Mistley Hall, a huge mansion, and the family has become exceedingly wealthy. He was also an MP who became Secretary for Ireland. Later he was elevated to Paymaster of the Forces, a cabinet-level post with responsibility for army pay, rations and logistics. It was considered to be one of the most lucrative government positions. The office holder could levy fees on a percentage basis on the monies he disbursed. 1776 was a busy time for the Paymaster. America had declared independence and large numbers of British troops were in America or en-route, backed up by a large naval force.

It was against this background that Rigby embarked on his dream of 'Mistley Spa', which would cost a fortune. Paymasters before him had left office very rich men. Rigby had no reason to believe he would be different. However there was disquiet in Government circles about financial irregularities within the Paymaster's office and other cabinet members were jealous. Contracts for building warships mysteriously found their way to the shipyards in Mistley and Rigby was well known as a spendthrift. He regularly held extravagant parties at his mansion. Furthermore he was under a cloud as he had amassed huge gambling debts and also because of his association with the *Naze Tower* scandal. This involved clandestine rendezvous between 'actresses' and gentlemen in high places at the then fashionable tea room in the *Naze Tower* at nearby Walton and was described as the perfect hideaway. Needless to say the term 'actress' was very loose in all senses of the word and the gentlemen were anything but. But it was all done in the name of theatre and promoting the arts! It might have remained quiet had not one of the actresses Martha Ray, been shot dead on the steps of Covent Garden Theatre in London by James Hackman, a clergyman.

In October 1781 the American war ended with the defeat of the British Army at Yorktown. Rigby's department was investigated by the House of Commons Commissioners of Public Accounts. Their report urged:

*"Immediate action to impose check on the money held at any one time by the Paymaster whilst in office, and to prevent those leaving office from taking large sums of public money with them".*

The investigators were not happy with the system in operation. It allowed the Paymaster (Rigby) to send the Treasury an estimate of monies needed for the army. The Treasury, without checking, would pay up with no questions asked. This arrangement had operated for years and consequently office holders had been able to acquire large sums of money. Rigby had been in the post for fourteen years. On leaving office Paymasters had simply pocketed the surplus balances and kept them until, or if, the accounts were finally approved. The previous Paymaster, Henry Fox, benefited from the use of public money for several years after he had left office. It took fifteen years for his accounts to be audited.

Richard Rigby resigned shortly after the Parliamentary commission reported and his funds were frozen. Finance for the Mistley Spa scheme dried up and the project ground to a halt. All that had been built were some lodges, the ornate fountain and a church, the core of which was later demolished, leaving the two still standing towers.

In April 1788, Rigby was somewhat astounded and embarrassed when he was requested to pay back a large sum of money to the public purse. This meant humiliation and disgrace and he died shortly afterwards leaving his estate and a host of problems to his sister and then his nephew, Colonel Hale Rigby. Not only did the government want its money back but a long line of personal creditors sought restitution, to say nothing of the vast expense in the upkeep of Mistley Hall and family houses in London.

Hale Rigby did his best to rectify the financial situation, however legal complexities and determined creditors made it almost impossible. He died in 1827 and the estate and all its problems were reluctantly inherited by John (the 4th Lord) Rivers, the great grandson of Richard Rigby's sister Martha. The situation was hopeless. The only solution was liquidation - the village of Mistley would be sold in lots at auction. For this parliamentary approval was required. It was quickly granted and the first auction began at noon on the 9th of August 1844. The great mansion of Mistley Hall was demolished the same year. There were further sales in September 1844 and two more in 1845. Everything went under the hammer, wharfs, shipyards, warehouses, farms, land, business premises, the hotel and inns, and even the Vicarage and Rectory.

The Rigby connection with Mistley had been severed. The two towers and the fountain are a reminder of what might have been.

# AT THE DOCTOR'S POND

*'We want an improved method of construction of a boat*
*That if filled with water will still stay afloat.'*

Just north of Great Dunmow town centre, on the Thaxted Road, next to the library, is the curiously named *'Doctor's Pond'*. A plaque on the railings erected during the Golden Jubilee in 2002 states *'legend has it that the name 'Doctor's Pond' is derived from a local doctor's use of the pond for breeding and keeping of leeches used in the medicine of the day'*. The doctor is not named and use of leeches frowned upon for 50 years by the National Health Service are now making a fashionable comeback.

However the pond's main claim to fame is that it is where Lionel Lukin first tested models of lifeboats. This too is mentioned on the plaque *'Lionel Lukin born Great Dunmow 18th May 1742 is famous for inventing the first 'unimerigible' lifeboat in 1784'*.

It is somewhat odd that Lukin chose building lifeboats as a quest since Great Dunmow is many miles from the coast and Lukin was neither seafarer nor boat builder. Lukin's business was making luxury coaches. He was described as having an inventive mind that liked a challenge. He was also well connected in high places, being acquainted with the Prince Regent and the Prime Minister William Pitt.

By 1785 Lukin had produced a prototype for which he obtained a patent. Further tests of full size boats were carried out on the Thames and in the sea near Ramsgate. His design incorporated water tight compartments and layers of cork to keep the boat afloat. Additional weighting was put on the keel to maintain stability. Lukin's designs were passed on to the Prince Regent but, in spite of encouragement and financial backing there was little interest from the Navy.

A few of the boats he built were sent to coastal towns for rescue work. In Bamburgh, Northumberland, one was used for many years as a lifeboat. Another was taken to Ramsgate, however this one appeared to have been used for less worthy causes - smuggling. In the same period other lifeboat designers were emerging and Lukin spent much of his time trying to stop his patent being copied.

In the age of sail it was not uncommon for vessels to get into trouble within sight of land in rough weather. In March 1789, the Collier Brig *'Adventure'* carrying coal was stranded on the Herd Sands, a shoal off Tynemouth a few hundred yards from the shore. Thousands of spectators on land watched helplessly as the ship foundered and the crew were drowned.

Such was the outrage following the tragedy, a reward was offered for the design of a boat *"to preserve the lives of seamen, from ships coming ashore"*. A local man, Henry Greathead, took up the challenge and produced a design considered a winner. He claimed the credit for the first lifeboat and was duly rewarded by a parliamentary grant of 1,200 guineas.

Meanwhile Lionel Lukin, when not engaged in litigation, had been working on other projects but eventually gave up due to failing eyesight. He retired to Hythe in Kent. On his death he asked for the following inscription to be put on his gravestone:

*"This Lionel Lukin was the first who built a life-boat,*
*and was the original inventor of that principle of safety,*
*by which many lives and much property have been preserved from shipwreck;*
*and he obtained for it the King's patent in the year 1785."*

Perhaps he asked for this memorial to set the record straight. It is not known where or when his rival Henry Greathead died or is buried. It is also not known what the other residents of Great Dunmow thought of a grown man playing with model boats at the Doctor's pond.

The National Lifeboat Institution was founded in 1824.

# GUNPOWDER'S LOT

The Crown acquired the Essex Gunpowder Mills at Waltham Abbey, straddling the River Lea on the County's border with Hertfordshire, in 1787. Prior to that date gunpowder was manufactured by private companies. The Army and the Navy were of the opinion that much of the gunpowder in use was substandard. Supply was inconsistent too. Stocks ran out when most needed as happened during the Dutch wars and the American Revolutionary conflict. Many of the private gunpowder makers had no particular loyalty to the nation, their main interest being turning in a profit. Following the disaster of the American War and with conflict again looming with the French, the British government decided, in effect, to nationalise most of the private factories. The Mills at Waltham Abbey were purchased from John Walton for £10,000 and thus The Royal Gunpowder Mills came into being.

Following acquisition the mills turned into, as might be said today, centres of excellence. This was achieved under the watchful eye of Sir William Congreve*, Deputy Comptroller of the Royal Laboratory at Woolwich Arsenal. New standards were set and rigorous quality control enforced. Manufacturing processes were upgraded to ensure continuous supply and substantial resources were allocated to research and development. The benchmarks of quality and cost established by The Royal Gunpowder Mills were then imposed on the remaining gunpowder makers in the private sector.

For over 200 years the mills remained under Government control with many innovations such as gun cotton, cordite, and the plastic explosive RDX being perfected there. Although the mills' main purpose was to provide for the military it was also a catalyst in the advancement of explosives for civil use.

With the industrial revolution in full swing, gunpowder related products were in great demand for tunnelling, mining and quarrying. During the First World War over 6,000 people worked in the Waltham Abbey factories. During World War II much of the production was dispersed due to the fear of enemy bombing. After the war work at Waltham Abbey resumed but concentrated on research such as rocket fuels and cartridges for firing jet aircraft ejector seats. Despite the innovative research the mills were gradually run down. The Waltham Abbey Mills turned full circle when what remained was privatised and the surplus land sold off to be developed for housing.

We should not leave the Gunpowder Mills without a tribute to the many terms commonly used today that have their origin in the early days of gunpowder.

In old naval days many phrases came to be
Such as some of the following as we shall see.
*A LOOSE CANNON* is perhaps someone out of control
or when the pitch of the sea could cause a gun to roll.
An unfair term maybe, but a bit of a rogue was the **SON OF A GUN**
The result of the parents on deck having their illicit fun.
Stuff the barrel was the master gunner's wish
using old rope - unwanted items or rubbish.
It was needed to stop a cannon ball falling into the sea,
So *A LOAD OF JUNK* found, was the key.
*FLASH IN THE PAN* was failure after a showy start.
It could be fatal in battle on the crew's part.
In which case **OVER A BARREL** was a situation helpless,
Or a crewman flogged for creating such a mess.
*HANG FIRE* – delayed an action.
Not always recommended as danger results from inaction.
Thus **STICK TO YOUR GUNS** and maintain your position
Don't change your mind, it's time to make a decision.
*BRASS MONKEYS* is a term for the extreme cold.
The brass racks would contract, the cannon balls no longer hold.
And **HOISTED BY ONE'S OWN PETARD** was the end
Blown sky high by the device made ready to defend.

The Royal Gunpowder Mills is now an industrial heritage attraction open weekends and bank holidays throughout the spring and summer months.

*Lieutenant-General Sir William Congreve (1743-1814) the Deputy Comptroller who first supervised the Gunpowder Mill should not be confused with his eldest son Sir William Congreve (1772-1828) who was an inventor and rocket designer who built rockets in a factory in Bow. (See Down the Lea Valley Page 164)*

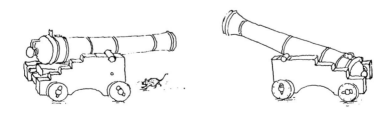

# JOHN CONSTABLE'S SCHOOL DAYS

*Every day young John would walk to school,*
*Observing the countryside as an absolute jewel.*
*Along the banks, across the fields or leafy lanes,*
*In snow or Summer's heat or wet from the rains.*

The River Stour, once the ancient barrier between the Angles and the Saxons, is now the boundary between Essex and Suffolk. From East Bergholt and Flatford on its north bank to Dedham village on its south, the countryside has been immortalised in the paintings of the area's most famous son, John Constable.

Constable was born in 1776, in East Bergholt, where his father, Golding Constable, was a prosperous miller and grain merchant. His parents were keen that he should receive a good education but he was unhappy at their initial choice of boarding school. They agreed that he complete his education as a dayboy at Dedham Grammar School. Every day for five years he walked the two to three miles from his home, along the river banks and through the countryside, of which he was later to say, *"I love every stile, stump and lane….these scenes made me a painter,"*

He was already painting and drawing regularly while at school and his headmaster, Dr Thomas Grimwood, once commented, after John's slowness in answering a question, *"Oh, John I see that you are in your painting room."* The school has long since been turned into a private house. It still stands in Dedham High Street and has a plaque over the door commemorating Thomas Grimwood.

On leaving school John worked in the family business. At the age of twenty-three, in 1799, his father made him an allowance to study art in London at the Royal Academy. His approach revolutionised landscape painting yet in spite of this he was not elected a full member of the Academy for another thirty years.

John Constable and his wife Maria came to stay in Leigh-on-Sea where he thought the air would be good for Maria's health. It was while staying at the house of his Uncle Thomas, sadly demolished in 1952, that he made sketches for his famous paintings of Hadleigh Castle. One of these may be seen in the Tate Britain gallery in London.

His paintings of the Stour valley, particularly of Dedham Vale, Dedham Mill, Flatford Mill, The Hay Wain and Willy Lott's Cottage, are now internationally recognised throughout the art world. This group depicts scenes that are still recognisable today. The Dedham Vale area is visited annually by thousands of tourists anxious to see for themselves the countryside he made so famous.

As his fame and reputation grew in the late nineteenth century this area of the Essex and Suffolk border became known as 'Constable Country.' It began to attract other artists. One of the most notable being the great equestrian painter Sir Alfred Munnings, who lived and worked in Dedham from 1919 until his death in 1959. His home at Castle House is now a museum and gallery dedicated to his life and work.

*Maldon was a big port, Chelmsford a small town.*
*Maldon didn't want a canal; afraid of trade going down.*

The idea of making the river Chelmer navigable was first mooted in 1677. It gained little support even though many of Chelmsford's needs came from the major port of Maldon involving lengthy, and costly, transport by pack mules or wagon and horses. In 1733 the cost of £9,355 was still too much and in 1763 £13,000 was also rejected. The people of Maldon were afraid of losing valuable port dues and trading monopolies

In 1793 however a new Act of Parliament approved a scheme, bypassing Maldon, for a canal from Heybridge Basin terminating at Springfield. In July of that year the new company, '*The Company of Proprietors of the Chelmer and Blackwater Navigation Limited*,' held their first meeting. In October John Rennie was appointed Director and Richard Coats day to day manager. They had worked together on the Ipswich to Stowmarket canal, and with the same team of experienced Suffolk navvies drove the canal through in record time to open fully in 1797.

The canal was a great success. Over a length of nearly fourteen miles there were twelve locks, 60 feet long by 16 feet wide to accommodate barges and lighters. In its busiest year, 1842, the canal carried sixty thousand tons of cargo. Sawmills, lime kilns, iron foundries, stone masons and coal merchants were just some of the industries that sprang up around the Springfield basin terminal.

In Chelmsford the first inland gasworks in Britain was built using coal brought by barge in 25 ton loads. A little downstream from Hoe Mill, Britain's first sugar refinery was established in 1832. The aptly named 'Paper Mill' located at North Hill, Little Baddow, was the first producer of paper in Essex. It gave its name to 'Paper Mill Lock' which was later to become the headquarters of the Proprietors of C&B.N (Chelmer and Blackwater Navigation) Ltd.

In 1843 the Eastern Counties London to Colchester Railway, built with materials mostly barged up from Heybridge, was completed. From then on there was a steady decline in traffic. Horsedrawn barges were replaced with motorised vessels in 1960 but 1972 saw the last commercial cargo on the canal. This was probably timber for Brown and Son, the Chelmsford Builders Merchants, a business begun by Richard Coats in the 1790s.

In 1978 the Navigation Company had sold all of its lighters and commissioned 'The Victoria' barge, a purpose built vessel 58ft long by 12' 6" wide and licensed to carry 48 passengers. This vessel may still be chartered for pleasure cruises and corporate functions and operates from Paper Mill lock.

The canal is still owned by the same company although it is now managed on their behalf by the Inland Waterways Association. The Chelmer Canal Trust Limited, a registered charity, is a voluntary group who also contribute to the wellbeing of the canal and its environs. Fishermen, canoeists and boating enthusiasts all use the canal and the towpath may be walked for the fourteen miles of waterway from Chelmsford all the way to Heybridge basin.

Undoubtedly the building of this navigable waterway was a major boost in the development of Chelmsford from a small market town to the bustling County Town that it is today.

# HARVEY'S SEA FENCIBLES

*"You are the First Sea Fencibles of Essex, every man.*
*Each and every one of you," Harvey barked most intense.*
*"Are our eyes and ears, essential for our coastal defence."*

**The Essex Sea Fencibles:** Probably the least known unit in the history of Britain's defences.

**HMS Temeraire:** A ship of war launched in 1798, built from oak cut in Hainault Forest, made famous in a painting by JMW Turner.

**The Battle of Trafalgar 1805:** England's most celebrated naval victory.

Three subjects with a common link: Sir Eliab Harvey of Rolls Park, Chigwell.

As the 18th century closed Britain was again embroiled in war with France. The threat of a seaborne invasion was very real. This led to the creation of a costal defence force known as the Sea Fencibles. The entire English coast facing the European mainland was covered by the scheme, as was Lands End and the whole shoreline up as far as Bristol.

The Sea Fencibles were a nautical Home Guard manned by part-time volunteers. Essex Sea Fencibles' zone began in Leigh-on-Sea in the south of the county and ran around the Essex shoreline to Harwich. The force comprised about 1500 men divided into small units, each serving their own community. Most of the volunteers lived in shacks on the coast and eked out a living from fishing and bait digging. One of the great advantages of joining the Sea Fencibles was that it exempted its members from being impressed into the navy. This was a boon for any man living near the sea. The fear of the navy's strong-armed press gangs turning up unannounced was very real.

Eliab Harvey's background couldn't have been more different from that of the average Sea Fencible. He was born into a privileged family at the huge Rolls Park estate which originally dominated much of Chigwell. Educated at Westminster and Harrow, he enrolled in the navy whilst still a pupil though he never went to sea whilst at school. When his elder brother William died suddenly, Eliab, just 21, inherited the estate plus a vast fortune.

The next year Eliab Harvey became MP for Maldon. Parliamentary duties didn't interrupt his naval career and after four years he resigned the seat. By the age of 35 he was in command of the '*Valiant,*' a 74-gun ship of the line, and saw action in the West Indies. Unfortunately Eliab contracted dengue fever in Jamaica which forced him to return home in late 1798.

Although still poorly, Harvey was sufficiently recovered to beg the Admiralty to find him something to do.

As going back to sea was out of the question, their ingenious solution was to offer him a part-time job as Captain of the Essex Sea Fencibles. For Harvey this arrangement was ideal. He could divide his time between recuperating at home in Chigwell and when required on field duties could stay in one of many comfortable lodgings scattered around the Essex coast.

Ideal it may have seemed but this command offered Harvey no excitement. The threatened invasion never materialised. The Fencibles were never called out in defence of the realm or took part in any meaningful action. It became apparent to Harvey that being in charge of a bunch of part-timers was quite different to life in the navy. The iron discipline that ruled a 'Man-o-War' could not be enforced on civilian volunteers. What the Fencibles thought of Harvey is not known.

Many of the Fencibles who lived around the Rivers Crouch and Blackwater were probably involved in smuggling in one form or another. They benefited enormously from the Navy's distribution of weapons and offers of sea combat and signals training. Furthermore volunteers were paid one shilling a day when they attended!

Harvey had fully recovered by the end of 1799 and was back at sea again. In 1803 he was appointed Captain of the *Temeraire*. When he later joined Nelson at the battle of Trafalgar, the *Temeraire* not only saved the day but also Nelson's ship the *Victory*, which had come under attack from the French ship *Redoubtable*. Today the *Victory* is preserved as a monument in Portsmouth's Royal Naval Dockyard.

The *Temeraire* survived until 1838 and would have been completely forgotten had it not been for the painter J.M.W. Turner. After witnessing the ship being towed up the Thames by a steam tug to be broken up, he produced 'The Fighting Temeraire', one of the nation's most famous paintings. Today this canvas hangs in the National Gallery in London.

As for Eliab Harvey he was promoted to Rear Admiral. Shortly afterwards he was, to all intents and purposes, dismissed from active service. He was accused of insulting his commander before the attack on Basque Roads in the Bay of Biscay. Harvey returned to his Rolls Park estate, his wife Louisa, their nine children and Parliament. He was still a hero to many and the public outcry at his treatment by the admiralty led to his reinstatement as a Rear Admiral. Harvey was eventually promoted to full Admiral although he never went to sea again.

With the threat of invasion over, the Essex Sea Fencibles faded into obscurity and was disbanded in 1810. It is presumed the volunteers returned to their previous way of life.

**Harvey's Sea Fencibles reporting for duty**

# TIMELINE

| ESSEX EVENT COMMEMORATED | YEAR | NATIONAL OR INTERNATIONAL EVENT |
|---|---|---|
| Nave of Chelmsford Church Collapses | 1800 | *Britain occupies Malta.* |
| Eliab Harvey becomes Captain of The Temeraire | 1803 | *Henry Shrapnel invents the Shell* |
| Temeraire and Harvey at Trafalgar | 1805 | *Battle of Trafalgar* |
| Sea Fencibles disbanded | 1810 | *First public Billiard room opens in Covent Garden* |
| | 1812 | *British PM Spencer Percival is assassinated in Parliament* |
| Elizabeth Fry visits Newgate Prison | 1813 | |
| Excavation of Bartlow Hills | 1815 | *Battle of Waterloo* |
| Hard Apple arrested on Goodwin Sands | 1820 | *Birth of Florence Nightingale* |
| John Constable paints Hadleigh Castle | 1829 | *Birth of Geronimo, Apache leader* |
| First Southend Wooden Pier opened | 1830 | *Last person put in pillory in England* |
| Machine Breakers Riot in Lt. Clacton | 1831 | *Belgium becomes independent* |
| Rotten Boroughs abolished | 1832 | *First Great Reform Act* |
| Alfred Lord Tennyson arrives in Epping | 1837 | *William IV dies, Victoria reigns.* |
| David Livingstone gets lost in Ongar | 1838 | *Public Record Office is established* |
| David Livingstone leaves for Africa | 1840 | *Queen Victoria marries Prince Albert* |
| Plum Puddings eaten at Romford Workhouse on Christmas Day | 1841 | *Britain claims sovereignty in Hong Kong* |
| Hockley Spa Pump Room Built | 1843 | *Dickens 'A Christmas Carol' published.* |
| Coggeshall Gang Strikes | 1844 | *YMCA founded in London* |
| Danbury Palace name adopted | 1845 | *Potato crop fails in Ireland* |
| HMS Warrior launched at Bow | 1860 | *Abraham Lincoln elected 16th US President* |
| Golden age of the Thames Barge | | |
| Death of Sarah Moore Leigh Sea Witch | 1867 | *Dominion of Canada created* |
| Southend Watch Vessel No 7 scrapped | 1870 | *Death of Charles Dickens* |
| Coalhouse Fort East Tilbury completed | 1874 | *Disraeli becomes Prime Minister* |
| Essex County Cricket Club formed | 1876 | *Wyatt Earp arrives in Dodge City* |
| Epping Forest Act Passed | 1878 | *First electric street lights in London* |
| William Morris writes on Walthamstow | 1883 | *Buffalo Bill creates 'Wild West Show'* |
| Essex Earthquake | 1884 | *General Gordon besieged at Khartoum* |
| A.C. Wilkin, founds Tiptree Jam | 1885 | *The Statue of Liberty arrives in USA.* |
| Rev. Baring-Gould writes Onward, CS | 1865 | *Abraham Lincoln is assassinated* |
| Transfer of Essex villages of Ugley, Farnham and others to Herts resisted. | 1888 | *Jack the Ripper murders six women in London* |
| Southend Iron Pier opened | 1889 | *Cecil Rhodes obtains royal charter for British South Africa Company* |
| Creation of Kynocktown | 1890 | *Death of Vincent van Gogh* |
| Salvation Army Colony opened in Hadleigh | 1891 | *Edison patents movie camera* |
| Marconi sets up in Chelmsford | 1895 | *Birth of Buster Keaton* |
| Gilbey Accolade for Finchingfield | 1898 | *Paris Metro opened* |

# GRAVE DIGGERS

*We rushed out to see what was going on*
*And saw the whole church roof had gone.*

Market day was held in Chelmsford every week outside the Shire Hall. Friday 17th January 1800 was a cold blustery day. Merchants from all over Essex had come to display their wares. As far as all were concerned everything was normal - all things considered. Once again the country was at war with their old enemy, the French, and the threat to the nation this time seemed severe. Napoleon, now master of most of Europe, had Britain firmly in his sights. Invasion fears were rife and the garrison stationed in Chelmsford outnumbered the town's population by nearly two to one.

In the early afternoon traders began to pack up before dusk fell. Close by, inside St Mary's Parish Church, workmen were chipping away around the stone pillars on the south arcade that held up the church roof. A vault was to be opened. The men were working as fast as they could. An internment was to be held early in the following week and they were not keen on working in a dark church when night had fallen.

By six in the evening all was quiet in the market place. A short walk away a dozen or so inns and taverns were doing a roaring trade - their doors pulled tight shut to keep out the winter cold. The raucous din generated within could not be heard in the churchyard. The quiet in the town centre was interrupted when the bells on the church tower chimed nine. Silence returned. Suddenly a resounding crash pierced the night air followed by an avalanche of breaking glass and snapping timbers. A chorus of madly barking dogs broke out. Horses whinnied and wildly kicked at their stable doors in the brewery on Duke Street. The merriment in the inns halted abruptly. The occupants nervously edged towards the door to peer out. In the pitch dark, and in the absence of street lighting, it was difficult to see anything. The air was thick with dust. Something terrible had happened.

With daylight the next morning a scene of utter devastation revealed itself in the church grounds. The columns of the south arcade had collapsed, bringing down the roof and parts of the north and south aisle. In the process the pews and the lower galleries had been smashed together with many icons and works of art. Like a sword poised to strike, a great sheet of lead hung precariously over the organ that had remained so far miraculously undamaged. Everything was coated in a thick layer of dust.

The 'Chelmsford Chronicle' even had difficulty summing up; - 'this stupendous ruin forms a scene of such awful and magnificent grandeur, words are inadequate to describe.'

Crowds of sightseers arrived and a young artist Samuel Nathan Summers (no known ancestor of the author) arrived with his stool, palette, paints and easel to capture the scene. Within a week the 'Chronicle' was carrying advertisements for engraved copies of his paintings which sold out rapidly.

A parish meeting was urgently convened and immediately authorised work to begin in shoring up the shattered church and retrieving the precious 'Hancock' organ. Within six months a Parliamentary bill had been passed authorising finance for re-building to go ahead. Three and half years later, on Sunday 18th September 1803, the newly restored church held its first service. It is remarkable how quickly the church was rebuilt. Considering the war, and economic depression that followed, perhaps it is even more amazing that all the loans were repaid within the 30-year schedule agreed back in 1800.

The 'Parish Church' became a Cathedral in 1914 when the Diocese of Chelmsford was created. Chelmsford Cathedral still holds one of the original 1801 bills for decoration – the repainting of the replacement Georgian gothic ceiling in Naples yellow - some 13 guineas.

The roof collapse was blamed on the careless 'grave diggers' working in the church that Friday afternoon. There are no records of what became of the men. We can only speculate what they were doing that evening. Perhaps they were enjoying themselves in one of the many inns, or simply tucked up in bed. Later they may have been recruited to help clear the damage or ironically even employed on the church rebuilding.

# THE LADY ON THE FIVE POUND NOTE

*Told of the horrors of women's prison life,*
*Elizabeth Fry, a good Quaker wife,*
*Went to see the women in Newgate jail*
*Crammed thirty to a cell with no hope of bail.*

Elizabeth Fry has adorned our £5 note since 1992 in recognition of her work in prison reform. She was born in Norwich in 1780 to wealthy, middle class Quakers, John and Catherine Gurney. In 1800 Elizabeth married Joseph Fry, the son of a successful Essex merchant family who were also Quakers, and came to live in the Fry family home in Plashet Park, now in East Ham.

In 1813, Elizabeth Fry, now a Quaker preacher and who had already given birth to eight children made her first visit to Newgate Prison* on the instigation of a family friend, Steven Gellet. As a child in Norwich, Elizabeth had accompanied her mother collecting clothes for the poor and visiting the sick. None of those experiences prepared her for the horrors of Newgate. She found women, and their children, living thirty to a cell in such squalor, filth and deprivation that she resolved to devote her energies to improving their lot.

During the next three years she organised friends to collect clothing for the inmates, had two more children and suffered the death of her daughter Betsy. By 1816, when she became a frequent visitor, with eleven other Quaker women she formed the, 'Association for the Improvement of the Female Prisoners in Newgate'. This group established a school, with a teacher elected from the inmates, and a chapel and regular Bible readings. They organised a system of supervision by matrons and monitors and provided materials for compulsory sewing duties where the women could make items to sell.

As a Quaker, Fry was opposed to the death penalty and campaigned vigorously for its abolition. At that time there were over two hundred offences, including the passing of forged notes and stealing clothing, which carried the death penalty.

Through her brother-in-law, Thomas Fowell Buxton the MP for Weymouth, she was invited to address the House of Commons. Whilst impressed with her charitable work, the majority of MPs believed that her views on capital punishment were misplaced. She pleaded with the Home Secretary, Lord Sidmouth, for the lives of two women condemned for forgery. He would not budge and warned Fry that her ideas were dangerous as they would, "remove the dread of punishment in the criminal classes".

She continued the campaign visiting prisons throughout the country, though prisons were not her only targets for reform. After seeing convicts being taken to the ships for transportation, in open carts with hand and leg shackles, she was successful in changing the way they were treated. She arranged for them to be taken in closed carriages to protect them from the missiles of the mob and the shackles were removed.

Visiting the convict ships became another regular duty for one of Fry's committees. Robert Peel, who succeeded Lord Sidmouth, and was more sympathetic, allowed many 'Fry inspired' improvements to be included in his '1823 Gaols Act'.

Another area that interested Fry was the training and standards of nursing. In 1840 she set up training courses at Guy's Hospital. Fry nurses were held in high esteem and Florence Nightingale was influenced by Fry's views on the training of nurses. She took a group of Fry nurses to the Crimea to nurse sick and wounded soldiers.

Queen Victoria, nearly forty years younger than Fry, was an admirer and supporter of her charitable work and they met on a number of occasions. The Queen wrote in her journal of Fry as, "a very superior person". Elizabeth Fry's influence was not confined to England. Towards the end of her life she travelled in Europe visiting many of the royal families to explain her work. In fact the King of Prussia visited the Fry family home and dined with her.

Elizabeth Fry died on 12 October 1845 after a short illness. It would be difficult to disagree with June Rose who says in her book, 'Prison pioneer The story of Elizabeth Fry';

> Over two hundred years after her birth, she seems a brave and modern woman, battling with the injustices of her time.

Her popularity may perhaps be measured by the fact that, although Quakers do not have funeral services, over one thousand people stood in silence as she was buried at 'The Society of Friends' graveyard in Barking.

* Newgate Prison closed in May 1902. The site was cleared for the new Central Criminal Court (Old Bailey) which opened in 1907. Most of the remaining women prisoners were transferred to Holloway.

# ONCE THERE WERE SEVEN

*Their Roman age secrets remained unseen*
*Until excavated in eighteen fifteen'.*

There are three remaining Bartlow 'Hills', lying just outside Ashdon in the north of the county. They were once part of the largest group of Roman barrows or burial mounds in Northern Europe. Their steep conical shape is typical of the Roman era and when built in the open countryside they took on the appearance of a range of small hills. Originally seven burial mounds were created and each contained a wealth of period materials and objects. For centuries the hills lay undisturbed, merely idle curiosities for locals.

In the 1700s, an awakening of interest in field archaeology led to the opening of Roman and Saxon burial mounds. As the Roman treasures in some mounds were revealed, the aspirations of those working for the benefit of science and history were ruthlessly pushed aside by others who saw financial gain.

Barrow digging became a sport that grew rapidly, often patronised by local squires desperate to furnish their houses with decorative relics. To some extent it was like the gold rush. Barrow diggers roamed the land indiscriminately digging up whatever they could find. Very often the methods used were shocking and more was destroyed in opening the site than was recovered. Rarely were any accurate records kept of what was found.

The Bartlow site came to the attention of the diggers in 1815, the year of the Battle of Waterloo, and was a typical example of the cavalier attitude prevalent at that time. Mr Busic Harwood, a retired Cambridge physician, turned up with a large party of men armed with the most rudimentary of tools and began excavations on the three taller barrows. He is quoted as saying *'my intention is to provide work for the unemployed'.* The party dug from the apex downwards. Exactly what Harwood and his men found is not known since the content unearthed simply disappeared without being recorded. It is suspected that all the 'loot' was shared out amongst the diggers who dispersed after the job was done.

Later excavations took place in April 1832, supervised by the historian John Gage of the Society of Antiquities. These digs were conducted in a much more scientific way and items recovered were logged and carefully stored.

Nevertheless, the opening of the remaining barrows took place in a carnival like atmosphere. The list of attendees the April dig attracted read like a 'Who's Who' of the locality.

A contemporary report records the attendance of Lord Maynard (later Viscount Maynard), the land owner, Lord Braybrooke, a neighbour, Professor Sedgewick, the Reverends Whelwell and Lodge, the Rectors of Ashdon and Bartlow respectively and several ladies and gentlemen from the locality together with their families, servants and workmen all dressed in their best.

The dig produced a number of relics, especially glass and china urns, a bronze lamp and the remains of burial caskets. After cataloguing they were removed for safekeeping to Easton Lodge in Dunmow, the family home of Lord Maynard. The barrows, now empty, were then left in peace although four of the smaller mounds were flattened during the construction of the Colchester and Stour Valley Railway in 1846.

A year later disaster struck when Easton Lodge caught fire and burnt to the ground, incinerating everything within. John Gage's dig did clear up one mystery. Previously it had been suspected that the 'Bartlow Hills' were burial mounds for Danish soldiers who died fighting the Anglo Saxons. Careful analysis by Gage identified the mounds as being Roman.

In 1978, overgrown and neglected, the Hills were taken into care by Essex County Council. They now lie just over the border from Essex in Cambridgeshire, following a minor boundary change in 1990.

A number of papers relating to the site excavation can be found in Saffron Walden Library and there are a few artefacts in Saffron Walden Museum.

# HARD APPLE

*William Blyth was a smuggler nicknamed 'Hard Apple'*
*With whom the Revenue for years tried to grapple.*
*A shopkeeper and Parish Councillor first rate,*
*He was also oysterman, constable and magistrate.*

Paglesham is one of the county's oldest fishing villages and William Blyth one of the most colourful characters from its past. Born in 1753, known to all as *'Hard Apple'*, he grew up to become a pillar of the community. During his 74 years he was the village grocer, parish councillor, churchwarden, constable and even magistrate, as well as being a successful oysterman. His marriage to Mary Dowsett linked his own large family to that of William Dowsett, fellow oysterman and notorious smuggler.

Paglesham Oysters were renowned for their quality and a good living was to be made from farming them. However, lucrative though it could not come close to the profits to be made from smuggling. Blyth and Dowsett, along with the Pagelsham families of the Embersons and the Wisemans, under cover of exporting oysters to the continent, made their village the smuggling capital of the East Coast.

Just how William Blyth came by the name of *'Hard Apple'* is not known though it is said that he was a man who feared nothing and lived life to the full and that drink had no effect on him. Although he had many encounters with customs officers according to their records he was never actually charged with anything.

Once when caught, his illicit cargo was taken aboard a revenue cutter. Blyth is then reputed to have begun drinking with the crew until they were drunk and incapable. He then transferred his cargo back to his own boat, plus contraband previously confiscated from other boats, thus showing a double profit on the day.

On another occasion he was arrested at sea and clapped in irons by the customs officer of Leigh, John Loten. When the revenue cutter ran aground on the Goodwin Sands Loten pleaded with Blyth to use his knowledge of the area to help them. Blyth is reputed to have answered, "I might as well drown as be hanged," but with the prospect of the vessel breaking up, in return for his freedom, he was persuaded to use his expertise to get them back to safe waters.

His exploits on land were just as outrageous. The nickname of *'Hard Apple'* may well have come from his reputation for hard drinking.

Once he was even said to have drunk two glasses of wine and then eaten the glasses he drank from! A keen cricketer, his team were once faced by a charging bull. *Hard Apple* promptly grabbed it by the tail and beat it with a cudgel. The beast took fright and with *Hard Apple* hanging on ran through a hedge, jumped over a ditch and dropped dead!

These exploits and many others were recorded by John Harriott in his memoir, 'Struggles Through Life', published in 1815. Harriott, a magistrate in nearby Great Stambridge, is credited with being involved in the founding of the Thames River Police, an organisation in which, surprisingly, one of William Blyth's sons later served. Harriott's tales have been often repeated by writers over the years and have led to *Hard Apple* becoming known as 'King of Smugglers,' although there were others even more active than him.

William Blyth died in 1830 and is buried in St Peter's Churchyard near 'The Punch Bowl', the scene of much of his legendary drinking. He lies next to his wife Mary, and two of his sons, Joseph and Daniel.

The efforts of the customs officers to stem the tide of contraband included the stationing of watch vessels in the river Roach. The most famous of these was the 'Beagle' notable for its voyages with Charles Darwin. In 1845 it was moored at the entrance to Pool Creek, just off 'Branfleet Spit' where the River Roach meets the Crouch.

Despite the best efforts of the authorities, smuggling, or free trade as the villagers preferred to call it, continued right up to the early twentieth century. However though the heyday of Pagelsham as its capital is long past, the character of William *Hard Apple* Blyth has earned a place in the history of this tiny village. His part in the folklore of Pagelsham is confirmed by his depiction on the current village sign, designed and built by local resident Rodney Choppen and erected in August 2000.

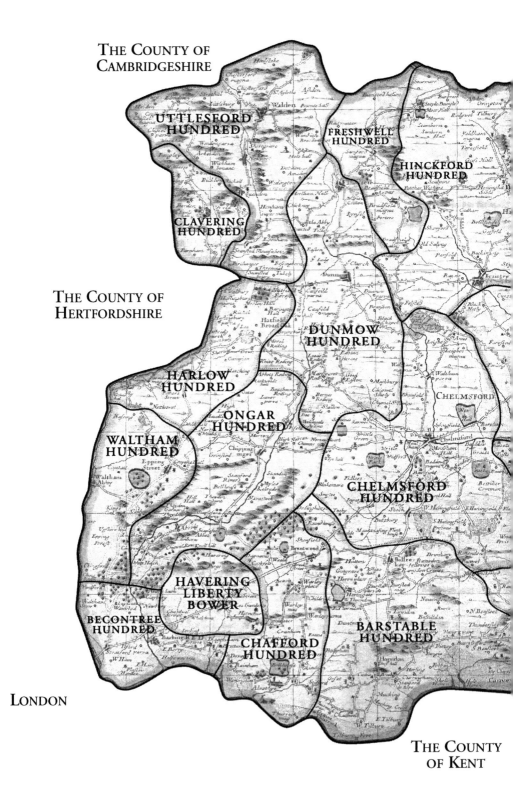

THE COUNTY OF
CAMBRIDGESHIRE

UTTLESFORD
HUNDRED

FRESHWELL
HUNDRED

HINCKFORD
HUNDRED

CLAVERING
HUNDRED

THE COUNTY OF
HERTFORDSHIRE

DUNMOW
HUNDRED

CHELMSFORD

HARLOW
HUNDRED

ONGAR
HUNDRED

WALTHAM
HUNDRED

CHELMSFORD
HUNDRED

HAVERING
LIBERTY
BOWER

BECONTREE
HUNDRED

BARSTABLE
HUNDRED

CHAFFORD
HUNDRED

LONDON

THE COUNTY
OF KENT

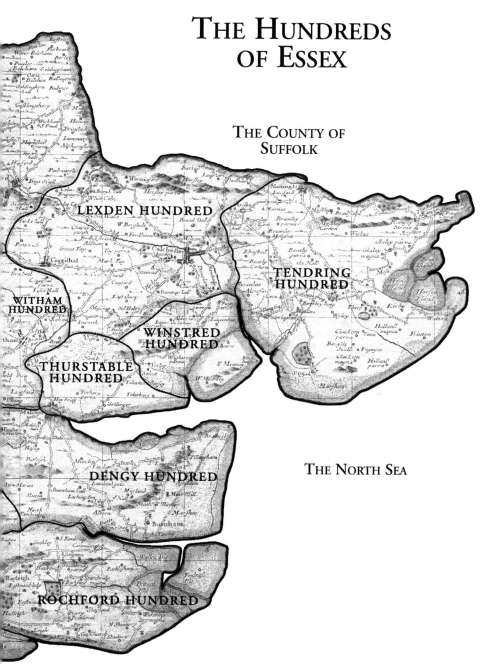

# THE HUNDREDS
# OF ESSEX

THE COUNTY OF
SUFFOLK

LEXDEN HUNDRED

TENDRING
HUNDRED

WITHAM
HUNDRED

WINSTRED
HUNDRED

THURSTABLE
HUNDRED

DENGY HUNDRED

THE NORTH SEA

ROCHFORD HUNDRED

THE RIVER THAMES

# CAPTAIN SWING

*All the protesters were long to remember*
*What took place on that eighth of December.*
*When in Little Clacton a mob did arise*
*That took the authorities quite by surprise.*

The Napoleonic wars were over. Many soldiers and sailors had returned home from years of service overseas. Times were hard and there was little in the way of civilian employment. History was seen to be repeating itself, whereby depression followed a great military victory. At the same time the industrial revolution was gathering pace which threatened the livelihoods of the already low paid agricultural workers. There was no obvious spark, just hearsay and rumour, but suddenly in 1830 much of rural southeast England was engulfed in a great wave of protest machine breaking.

On 7th December a mob of 150 ran riot in Great Clacton and caused a great deal of property damage. Two days later a similar sized group, fuelled by drink, assembled in the dead of night in Little Clacton with the express purpose of seeking out and destroying a thrashing machine kept in a locked barn there.

The leader of the rioters was a so called *'Captain Swing'* who supposedly took his name from the 'swing' or moving part of the flail used to thrash the grain. The rioters, in turn, were collectively referred to as *Swing Rioters*. After the protest died down, the authorities moved swiftly and showed little mercy in pursuing the ring leaders and their associates. Fifty Essex men from Clacton were charged with a variety of offences. Nationally some 2000 men and women were convicted and over 500 were transported to Van Diemen's Land (now Tasmania, Australia) to serve between 5 and 14 year terms.

One local man, Benjamin Hackshall, made a futile attempt to escape arrest, first by hiding up a neighbour's chimney for days, then fleeing to London. However he was apprehended on New Year Day by a 'Bow Street Runner'.* Luckily for him he escaped transportation. After having served a relatively short spell in Chelmsford jail, he returned to his family in Little Clacton. Hackshall then became a minor celebrity by composing a popular ballad, which gave a romantic account of the riots.

Five years later in February 1835, 200 of those convicted and transported received free pardons, although most chose to stay in Australia.

---

*\* The Bow Street Runners were so called because they were based at Bow Street magistrates' court in London. As they didn't wear uniforms they were considered the forerunners of the modern day CID (Criminal Investigation Department).*

## SAD DAYS AT HIGH BEECH

*My sleep is restless and I feel my power ebbs away.*
*The forest trees hem me in and keep me at bay.*

Alfred, Lord Tennyson is one of England's most celebrated poets. Born in 1809, on his death at 81 he was buried in poets' corner at Westminster Abbey. His best remembered poem *The Charge of the Light Brigade* was published in 1855 as a memorial to the suicidal charge of the British light cavalry at the Battle of Balaclava in the Crimean War a year earlier.

Tennyson was twenty when he won the Chancellor's Gold Medal at Trinity College Cambridge. He left Cambridge, without taking his degree, in 1831 on the death of his father

In 1833 Tennyson published his second book of poetry. Some critics of the day revelled in the severity of their critical reviews. This hurt Tennyson badly, so much so he published nothing further for nine years although he continued to write. In the same year he was traumatized by the sudden death of his friend Arthur Hallam at the age of 22.

In 1937 Tennyson became engaged to his childhood sweetheart, Emily Sellwood. Soon after, the Tennyson's moved to High Beech House on the edge of Epping Forrest, while Emily was left in Lincolnshire. Tennyson spent three years at High Beech with his mother, generally feeling sorry for himself. He wrote often to Emily saying how he missed her and how awful life was at High Beech. Emotionally and financially these were difficult years for Tennyson. He claimed he could not even afford the train fare to visit Emily. Suffering from depression, he stayed for two weeks as a guest in Dr. Matthew Allen's High Beech Asylum. He reported that mad people were *the most agreeable and most reasonable persons* he had met. Tennyson would later regret the acquaintance of Dr. Allen. Whilst apparently not having money for a train fare he managed to invest his family's money in a woodcarving scheme of the Doctor's and lost everything. As a consequence plans to marry Emily were postponed again.

If High Beech and Epping Forest provided a setting to match Tennyson's mood it was a productive one. It was here that he began writing his epic poem *In Memoriam,* a tribute to his friend Arthur Hallam. It took him 17 years to write. Within two years of leaving Essex for Tunbridge Wells, in 1840, he published two volumes of *Poems,* which met with immediate success.

This was the beginning of real recognition for Tennyson. In 1850 he married Emily, was created Poet Laureate and published *In Memoriam* to universal acclaim. The next forty years produced a body of work that has made him the second most frequently quoted writer after Shakespeare. It would appear that, for all the sadness Tennyson felt in Essex, his stay there was a significant turning point on his road to greatness.

# LOST IN ONGAR

*At Stanford Rivers the fog had grown thicker*
*He climbed a lamppost to see which road would be quicker*

At the age of 27, the famous explorer and missionary Doctor David Livingstone went to Africa. He travelled down the great Zambezi River to discover *'The Smoke that Thunders,'* which he renamed Victoria Falls after the then Queen. Two years before his death, after a long search, the journalist Henry Morgan Stanley met Livingstone in 1871 with the famous phrase, *Doctor Livingstone I presume.* During his 30 years in Africa Livingstone crossed the continent from the Atlantic to the Indian Ocean, in the process walking some 5,000 miles. Although he died in Africa, his body was brought to England to be interred in Westminster Abbey.

A self-educated Scot from Blantyre, Livingstone trained as a doctor in Glasgow. In 1838 he was accepted as a probationer by the 'London Missionary Society'. He was then sent to study under the Rev. Richard Cecil in Chipping Ongar. He lodged with other students in what are now called the 'Livingstone Cottages' in Ongar High Street. During that time his colleague and fellow probationer Joseph Moore recorded an incident, which, in view of his future achievements was surprising to say the least.

One November day David Livingstone set off on foot to London to visit a sick relative, a round trip of some fifty miles. Fellow students marvelled at the energy and drive that would be needed to walk this distance. Later in the day Dr Livingstone returned via Edmonton. There is a story that he stopped to render assistance to a lady who had fallen off her horse but this cannot be verified. However, with night falling and a thick fog descending, the Doctor lost his way at Stanford Rivers not far from Ongar. Naturally by this time he felt weary and footsore. After some time walking round in circles he managed to find a lamppost on which he climbed and managed to get his bearings. Eventually, with the clock striking 12 midnight, David Livingstone made it back, much to the relief of his fellow students. Nevertheless he was ribbed mercilessly in the following days. Was the experience of getting lost on a 50-mile walk in Essex adequate preparation for a 5,000-mile walk across uncharted Africa? It hardly bears thinking about.

# CHRISTMAS DAY IN THE WORKHOUSE.

*At Romford Union Workhouse then*
*Imagine the furore*
*When on Christmas day plum puddings*
*Were given to the poor.*

Prior to 1834 each parish had to take care of its poor. Romford was no exception and the amount of the poor rate was always a bone of contention for those that paid it. For the workhouse inmates, their Christmas diet was like any other day, the extra expense of seasonal fare being considered unacceptable.

The Romford Poor Law Union, formed in 1836, brought the poor of ten parishes; Barking, Cranham, Dagenham, Hornchurch, Havering-atte-Bower, Rainham, Romford, Upminster, Great Warley and Wennington, under the responsibility of one Board of Guardians. With the new organisation came some enlightened thinking. Within three years the board had bought a five acre site at Oldchurch and built a 'state of the art' new workhouse with a capacity for 450 people. The 'enlightened thinking', to some of the public, may have been a step too far when, in 1841, there appeared a report in the Essex Standard stating that, 'On Christmas day, the 400 inmates had been given 240 plum puddings, with a total weight of 600 lbs'. The Guardians withstood the criticism of wasting ratepayer's money and the practice of allowing inmates to celebrate Christmas like this was established for future years.

The workhouse of necessity had its own infirmary. In time it came to treat not only the residents but also the poor generally. This aspect of its work gathered such a reputation that, in 1893, a hospital was added. Experience gained by the staff during and after the Great War led to its recognition as a respected medical institution. In 1924 the hospital was expanded becoming bigger than the workhouse itself.

The Poor Law Union was dissolved in 1930, the institution being taken over by Essex County Council. In 1935 responsibility for Oldchurch Hospital was given to the Public Health Committee. It was much enlarged and grew to become a major regional hospital and a nationally respected centre of expertise in Neurosurgery. In 2000 the hospital was closed and replaced by a new hospital built close by.

Of the old Victorian buildings the last part of the central cruciform block, a highlight of the original Francis Edwards design, was dismantled to make way for a car park. The remaining buildings still standing at the time of writing are derelict. Whether any will be preserved depends on the Guardians of today, The London Borough of Havering and its development partners.

# HOCKLEY SPA

*For London, Essex waters had become all the rage*
*All digestive problems they were said to assuage.*

The belief that taking mineral waters or bathing in spa waters was a cure for all sorts of human ailments has been around for hundreds of years. However life style remedies tend to go round in circles. What is fashionable today is suddenly out of favour tomorrow. In spite of this there has been no end of candidates willing to try their luck and risk all their money, or someone else's, in spa ventures.

The great spa towns in England such as Bath, Buxton and Harrogate have all had ups and downs. Bath Spa recently re-opened but it has taken years to rebuild and cost in the region of £26 million. As we have shown earlier (page78) Richard Rigby, a minister of the crown, spent much of his own fortune, and apparently considerable amounts of taxpayers money on a private project to create a grand spa town in Mistley on the River Stour. It ended in financial disaster and disgrace for Rigby.

In the 1830s the small village of Hockley became the centre of a spa project, although less grandiose than Mistley. Robert and Leticia Clay moved to Hockley from Cheltenham (another spa town) in the hope that the fresh Essex country air would relieve Mrs Clay's persistent asthmatic cough. Within a short time Mrs Clay's condition had improved dramatically and she concluded that this was mainly due to drinking water drawn from a well at the back of the house. The well was described as 10 feet deep with a constant source of water. It never ran dry in the severest droughts or froze in the coldest of weathers. On analysis the water was said to contain *Epsom Salts.*

Within a short space of time Mrs Clay had set up a 'Spa', run from her own house, and was extolling the virtues of the waters. A long list of cures were claimed for all sorts of ailments such as asthma, coughs, rickets, arthritis, headaches and disorders of the blood. Mrs Clay's recommended solution was to drink one and a half pints of water at least four times a day straight from the well. So successful was Mrs Clay with her marketing that the business came to the attention of investors in London.

In 1843 a London solicitor, appropriately named Henry Fawcett of Fawcett and Co., assumed control of the business and engaged the services of well-known architect James Lockyer. This resulted in a new pump room being built further down Spa Road and the construction of the present day Spa Hotel. The pump room was created in the form of a Grecian temple.

Within this structure floor to ceiling mirrors lined the walls and impressive chandeliers hung from the ceiling. There were elegant marble fireplaces at either end of the main room. No expense was spared on the new hotel which was considered exceedingly luxurious.

Alas, the anticipated great throng of visitors never materialised. There were no bathing facilities and, much to Fawcett's dismay, the clientele, as well as having the desire to take the waters, wanted day and night time entertainment. Sadly Hockley could not supply what was available in the big Spa towns like Bath and Harrogate.

There was more misfortune for the new owners. The Spa's completion in the 1850s coincided with the opening of the London to Southend railway. Londoners, potentially the Spa's biggest customers, could now get to Southend quickly to indulge in the new fad of sea bathing. For some years Hockley Spa struggled on. A daily delivery service of bottled water to London by cart was introduced. This failed however, ruined by unsubstantiated rumours of contamination.

In 1873 the pump room, long since closed, was leased as a Baptist chapel. Later it became a billiard room. During the 20th century it saw service as a tea-room, a shirt factory, and in the manufacture of billiard tables. Much of the time it was closed and served as a store. The pump room is now a private dwelling. The present owners have retained the exterior façade and are in the process of renovating the interior.

# THE COGGESHALL GANG

*"The 'Coggeshall Gang' as they came to be known*
*Were a blot on the history of that peaceable town."*

The Essex Standard of June 1838 reported that, *For some time past the neighbourhood of Coggeshall has been infested with a gang of housebreakers, who have carried out their work in a most audacious manner.* It was to be another ten years before the perpetrators of these crimes, and worse to come, were brought to justice.

The Essex Constabulary was formed in 1840. The force in Witham consisted of a superintendent, Charles Cooke, supported by two constables plus a further two officers stationed at Coggeshall. The activities of this gang were to be a tough test for them particularly between 1844 and '48. It was during this four-year period that what amounted to a reign of terror descended on the Coggeshall area through the appalling violence which accompanied the burglaries.

If the gang had a headquarters it was probably the 'Black Horse Inn' where William French, half brother to the gang's leader, Samuel Crow, was the landlord. He, it transpired, was the fence through which the stolen goods were dispersed. The rest of the gang was made up of ten to fourteen men. Crow was well placed to identify likely targets for them. He was a well-known driver of post chaises for innkeepers of the area and the local gentry.

In 1844 the unoccupied home of Charles Skinner in Coggeshall was burgled. Only a quantity of wine was stolen but the thieves then burned his house down. In 1845 the 'Bird in Hand' pub in East Street and the grocer, Richard Bell's, warehouse were burgled as well as many private houses. In one of these the owner was threatened with a pistol and nearly suffocated under a mattress whilst the gang drank his wine before stealing his gold and silver.

Things reached crisis level when four members of the gang broke into the house of James Finch and his housekeeper. They were both held over an open fire to make them tell where their money was kept, the housekeeper being seriously burned when her clothes caught alight. James Finch had a rope tied round his neck and nearly died when hauled up to a rafter. Ignoring their victims the thieves ate and drank before escaping with £6 and all the provisions they could carry.

The police were getting nowhere until in 1847 a constable caught one of the gang, William Wade. He was convicted and while in Chelmsford prison awaiting transportation he had a disagreement with Samuel Crow who visited him. Wade informed on the gang and arrest warrants were promptly issued. The criminals fled or went into hiding but the police, now armed with names, were hot on their trail.

Two of them, Payne and Whittaker, were arrested on board a steamer about to leave Liverpool for New York. The leader, Samuel Crow, was eventually arrested aboard another steamship the 'James Watt' bound for Hamburg.

The rest of the gang were caught within the county and brought to trial at Chelmsford Essex Assizes in March 1849. Samuel Crow, William Tansley and William 'Crusty' Ellis were sentenced to transportation for life for their assault on James Finch. Crow died in prison before the sentence was carried out however his fifteen-year-old brother received three months hard labour for helping him in a bid to escape. William Wade received fifteen years transportation, reduced to seven because he had turned Queen's evidence. Other active gang members were also transported for seven years. The Gang were lucky to be sentenced to transportation. A hundred years earlier they may have been hanged like that other infamous Essex man, Dick Turpin, whose terrorising methods were very similar (see page 68, Stand and Deliver).

Through the 'falling out of thieves' - the argument between Wade and Crow - and the doggedness and perseverance of the Essex Constabulary, the reign of terror that had blighted Coggeshall was at an end.

## LAUNCH OF THE WARRIOR

*The First Lord smashed a bottle of wine over her bow.*
*"God speed the 'Warrior' - your time is now"*

In 1860, December was one of the coldest for 50 years. Frozen snow covered the shipyard and icicles hung like daggers from roofs and pipes. Frost encrusted cranes sparkled as if decked in gems. Bow Creek was thick with ice. Against this backdrop, the Thames Iron Works, just inside Essex, was to be the setting of not just a national first but an international one too. It was the 29th of the month and hundreds of braziers blasted out heat as two thousand men worked like demons to ensure the vessel would be ready on time. Crowds of spectators of all ages, including old men and young babies wrapped against the winter's chilling bite, grew by the hour. Soon there would be thousands scrambling to find a vantage point. Inside the dock the hull of the *Warrior* rose tall. Every launch from the shipyard was an event in itself but this one was going to be a celebration of national pride and triumph.

Sir John Pakingham MP stepped up to perform the launch ceremony; the *Warrior* however refused to move. Despite dozens of burning braziers placed close to the hull, slipway steel remained frozen to iron keel. Tugs were called in to give extra leverage and shipyard workers on the upper deck ran from side to side trying to rock the vessel free. After 20 minutes, and accompanied by a great cheer, the *Warrior* finally broke away and eased down the slipway.

The launch heralded a new chapter in maritime history. At a stroke all existing warships became out of date. The *Warrior's* vital components, main guns, engines and boilers were encased inside an armoured iron hull. The revolutionary design offered power from both steam and sail. New breech-loading guns and a powerful engine meant that the ship could outrun and outgun all others. At 10,000 tons it was one of the biggest ships afloat. It was remarkable that a vessel of such size could be launched in the confined area of Bow Creek. By way of comparison the *Warrior* is almost the same size as the World War II cruiser *HMS Belfast* that is permanently moored in the Thames opposite the Tower of London.

For a time the Thames Iron Works was the most important shipyard in the country. During the 75 years of its life, until it closed in 1912, over 600 ships were built - from small cutters to great dreadnoughts. At its peak 7,000 workers were employed. The navies of Japan, Portugal, Sweden and Germany featured prominently in its order book. One ship, the cargo-passenger-gunboat *Yavari*, was even crated up in kit form and sent to Lake Titicaca, 2 miles above sea level in Peru, where it was to be assembled! Mules were used to carry the ship's sections on the last leg of the journey up the high mountain passes to get to the lake.

Most traces of the once mighty ship yard have now disappeared. The slip ways and buildings have long gone and the site is cut in two by the lower River Lea road crossing. At the entrance to Canning Town station, on the edge of the former shipyard is an inscription carved in concrete by Richard Kindersley that gives a potted history.

Nevertheless the Thames Iron Works legacy lives on. West Ham United Football Club (The Hammers) had its origins in the yard's social club. Crossed hammers like those used in ship construction appear on the club's logo. Should the reader care to travel further afield - to Peru and onwards to Lake Titicaca - the *Yavari* is still there. It claims to be the oldest surviving single propeller iron ship that remains in working order.

We started with the *Warrior* so that is where we will end. Within a decade of the launch the ship was obsolete. Never once had it fired a shot in anger and it soon fell victim to rapidly evolving warship technology. In 1883 the ship was withdrawn from sea service, stripped and used as a depot ship. Worse was to follow. The *Warrior* was sold and for 50 years it served as a floating oil jetty at Pembroke Dock in Wales, renamed *Oil Fuel Hulk C77*. In August 1979 the Maritime Trust rescued The *Warrior* and took it to Hartlepool to begin a restoration process estimated to take 8 - 10 years and cost up to £10 million. In 1860 the cost of building the *Warrior* including guns and initial coal supply was £390,000. Today the fully restored *Warrior* can be seen in Portsmouth harbour close by that other legend of British naval history - Nelson's *Victory*.

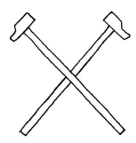

**The Hammers**

# THAMES BARGE

*Out there she lies, sedately on the tide,*
*A legacy of dim-departed seas*

Every day hundreds of heavy goods vehicles thunder along the roads of Essex taking goods into London and beyond. Comparisons between a 40-ton truck and a Thames sailing barge may seem absurd. Yet 100 years ago the sailing barges, on the waterways of Essex and into the capital, were the HGVs of the day, carrying the essentials to build, repair, fuel and feed the capital. Today there are about 30 seaworthy sailing barges left; they are used for recreation, charter work and racing. Once at least 5000 such vessels worked in and around Essex, making a magnificent sight as they glided gently by with their tan sails framed in the rich colours of the setting sun. H. Rider Haggard captures their ability to penetrate far inland in his 1902 book 'Rural England', *On the distant deep some sails and in the middle marsh, a barge gliding up a hidden creek as though she moved across a solid land.*

The barges, with their shallow draft, were robust and relatively inexpensive to build. Their ability to take large and bulky cargoes made them cost effective. A familiar sight were the hay barges with hay stacked 12 or even 20 feet high*; one man stood on top passing instructions to the other at the tiller who could not see where he was going. It was common for just two people to sail a barge carrying 100 tons of cargo. To carry similar loads on land would have required a hundred horse-drawn carts plus one hundred drivers!

Thames Barges were a development of craft that had been around since medieval times. The first Essex sailing barge was built in Rettendon in 1791, records would suggest, and the last in Mistley in 1928. The Thames Barges came of age during the Napoleonic Wars, survived and even expanded through the advent of steam.

The golden age of the Thames Barge was the early to mid 1800s. This was also the great era of railway building, which eventually would be the barge's biggest competitor. Ironically it was often the barges that carried the materials to strategic points, thus speeding railway construction and, from 1860 onwards, their own gradual decline.

In the First World War sailing barges made significant contributions to supplying the troops and in the Second World War they played a key part in the evacuation of Dunkirk.

After the First World War the decline of sea-going, cargo carrying barges accelerated. New maritime safely standards were introduced that required additional crew.

In some instances the owners were reluctant to fit auxiliary engines, as this would cost money to fuel them. In the end the barges could not compete with the modern alternatives, namely the articulated truck that is so familiar on the county's roads today. Notwithstanding this there were still barges carrying commercial cargoes when Neil Armstrong set foot on the moon.

*The so called stackies carried hay from the country side to London to feed the capital's horses which were used to pull the carriages and buses of the time. In many cases the return cargo was what was described as the 'London muck'. In the next chapter we encounter the Reverend Baring Gould who was not best pleased about this cargo.*

# ONWARD, CHRISTIAN SOLDIERS

*The opening lines of the immortal hymn*
*Written by the Rector of East Mersea on a whim.*

"It's bleak and inhospitable - the ends of the earth. I cannot say that I either liked the place or became attached to the people. The peasants were dull, shy and suspicious, I never managed to understand them. The dialect is markedly vulgar and the children of the parish uncouth. There were no resident gentry. As far I could see there were not many persons of value with whom to make friends. Then there was the London muck*- the stench was horrible - and the swarms of mosquitoes… "

Comment like this normally provokes outrage in the local community and especially more so if made by one its leading members: the Rector! Yet, over 125 years later, these comments of the Reverend Sabine Baring-Gould were affectionately quoted in local guide books for East Mersey. Baring-Gould arrived at East Mersey on March 21st 1871 as the new Rector of the Church of St Edmund. His comments cannot have endeared him to his parishioners though his description of the island as the ends of the earth may be understandable. During his tenure there was no proper road connection to the mainland and crossing, in winter, in the dark was a risky business. Until the end of the First World War nearly all of the island's essentials were brought in by boat as was the 'London muck' .

Baring-Gould and his wife Grace had a large family, they would eventually have fifteen children, and had outgrown the accommodation at Dalton near Thirsk, where he was Rector. They moved from Yorkshire to Essex after the Prime Minister, William Gladstone, confirmed his appointment at St Edmund's.

The Rector had already achieved some celebrity status with the publication of his hymn Onward Christian Soldiers which he said was written in ten minutes. Although he mused; the rhymes were faulty and not well based, he completely ignored changes suggested by the church hierarchy. Nevertheless the hymn was an instant success and has become one of the best known rousing evangelistic hymns.

Baring-Gould was a prolific writer completing over 100 booklets and 30 novels in his lifetime. Once, in the British Library, there were more books bearing Gould's name than any other English writer. One reason mooted for his leaving Yorkshire was that he needed a new challenge and the post on Mersea Island offered plenty of scope for new writing material.

On arrival in Essex, the Reverend began writing one of his most compelling fictional works 'Mehalah', the tragic story of a beautiful girl 'Glory' and the violent tempered Elijah Rebow. It is based on local characters and set against a backdrop of their grim surroundings. The author spared no effort in describing the dull and desperate lives of his creations and their surroundings. 'Mehalah' was first published in 1880 and is still in print. Being so busy with his writing and tending to the needs of his large family, it is questionable how much pastoral care the Rector could give to the parishioners of East Mersea. Whether his flock appreciated being portrayed as characters in the novel 'Mehalah' is debatable too.

After 10 years in Essex, Sabine Baring-Gould moved again, this time back to his native Devon. On the death of his uncle, he inherited the family home, Lew Trenchard Manor, northwest of Dartmoor. There he continued to write and preach until his death at the age of 89 in 1924.

Today, looking south across the River Blackwater, the grey brooding towers of Bradwell's now closed nuclear power station offer a certain dignity to the skyline. Unlike in Baring-Gould's day, modern utilities are now available and the 'London muck' no longer arrives. However, with the exception of boat users, getting on and off Mersea Island can still present a challenge. There is only one access road which runs south from Colchester and connects to the island by what is known as the Strood, a sea level tarmac road crossing. During the higher spring tides the Strood is covered by water and becomes impassable except for vehicles with high ground clearance.

* London muck. These were the Reverend Sabine Baring-Gould's very own words. He described them it in great detail as the 'sweepings of London streets' collected in the age of horse drawn transport. The 'muck' was brought on a daily basis from the capital by Thames Barge and used as manure on the fields.

# THE SEA WITCH

*She foretold the sex of the unborn child*
*And could say what the future would hold.*
*To upset her would risk a terrible curse*
*That might last for generations to come.*

Many parts of Essex have been associated with witches and witchcraft. Matthew Hopkins, the 'Witchfinder General,' is remembered in Mistley for his dreadful persecutions in the 17th century. Rochford Hundred has seen its fair share of the occult with people like George Pickingale in Canewdon and 'Cunning' Murrell of Hadleigh. In 1998 the opening of 'The Sarah Moore' pub in Leigh-on-Sea commemorated the town's infamous 'Sea Witch', as Mother Moore became known in the 19th century.

In mid-Victorian times Sarah Moore lived in a tiny cottage off Victoria Wharf in what is now known as Leigh Old Town. From contemporary accounts she looked the archetype witch, weather-beaten and toothless, with a hooked nose and a harelip. If appearances were not enough she had a mean disposition and most people would try to avoid upsetting her.

Sheila Pitt-Stanley, in her book, 'Legends of Leigh,' quotes personal evidence of the Sea Witch affecting her family. In 1850 her great-great grandmother, Eliza, expecting her third baby, was confronted by Sarah Moore, offering to tell the sex of the unborn child. Her brusque refusal resulted in the retort; *you're worried about having one more mouth to feed ain't yer? But mark my words, not one mouth, but two mouths....and my mouth it will be.* At this Eliza slapped her face, only to be cursed that her female line would forever bring up their children alone. Pitt-Stanley relates that her ancestor did indeed give birth to twins born with the harelip, the mark of the Sea Witch. Also that, since 1877, succeeding generations of her female line have had to bring up their children alone.

There are many legends of Sarah Moore's misdeeds. On the anniversary of her son's death from cholera, in a jealous rage she cursed five babies in the town and all died within three weeks. These deaths are born out by the parish register: the curse or coincidence? The most legendary tale of the Sea Witch must be that which marked her death. A skipper refusing to *buy a fair wind* laughed at her. Boarding his boat he was no sooner out at sea than a great squall blew up catching the boat which keeled over. One of the crew cried, *it's the witch!* The Skipper, fearing that the rigging would take them down, grabbed an axe and shouting, *I'll kill that witch!,* struck the rigging three times. On the third stroke the storm ceased abruptly and the boat was able to limp home. Approaching Leigh they were horrified to see the slumped figure of the Sea Witch, dead, from what looked like three blows of an axe.

# SOUTHEND WATCH VESSEL NO 7

*Watch Vessel Number Seven, no more to function.*
*Sold for salvage, destined for destruction.*
*Abandoned on the banks of the River Roach*
*Now lies deep in the mud of Pagelsham Reach.*

Beginning life as HMS Beagle, Southend Watch Vessel No 7, a Cherokee Class, 10-gun sailing ship, was launched from Woolwich in 1820. They were nicknamed 'Coffin Brigs' in the navy, because 26 of the 107 built were lost at sea. Beagle, however, after being kept in reserve for five years, was refitted as a survey ship and made a four-year voyage to South America surveying Patagonia and Tierra Del Fuego. In 1831, Captain Robert Fitzroy invited the 22 year old Charles Darwin to be the expedition naturalist on what became known as *The Voyage of The Beagle*. This epic five year voyage is mostly remembered for Darwin's observations, which led to his theories on evolution, published as *'On The Origin Of Species'* in 1859. The Beagle's last survey was to Australia under command of John Wickham. She left Plymouth in 1837 and did not return for six years. Shortly after this successful voyage HMS Beagle was transferred, in 1845, to the Customs and Excise service.

Renamed 'Southend Watch Vessel No 7' the vessel was used in anti-smuggling patrols along the Essex coast. An 1847 chart shows it moored in the River Roach. There it played a part in intercepting smugglers bringing in contraband along the maze of rivers, channels and creeks that criss-crossed East Coast Essex. Moved ashore to a fixed mooring in 1850, the Beagle became the home of customs officers and their families. The last known record of the vessel, dated 1870, is that it was sold for scrap for £525.

Its whereabouts remained a mystery until in 1997 Professor Colin Pillinger of the Open University proposed a plan for a space capsule to land on Mars. Accepted by the European Space Agency the project became known as 'Beagle 2,' commemorating Darwin's voyage of discovery. Pillinger asked marine archaeologist, Dr Robert Prescott from St Andrews University, to help local researchers in searching for the original HMS Beagle.

In 2004, a research team led by Prescott using ground penetrating radar, and with technical help from the Mars Beagle 2 team, located what they believe to be the remains of HMS Beagle. Her last resting place would appear to be in a sunken dock, covered in four to five meters of mud, on the banks of the River Roach close to Potton Island. The discovery suggests that the bulk of the ship is intact and in theory could be raised and restored. More research is required to confirm this and if it were to happen, as Robert Prescott has said, *The Beagle is a historic icon and would make a superb centre of scientific pilgrimage.*

# COALHOUSE FORT

*The big black guns were tried and tested in thin air,*
*But not a shot was fired in war.*

For over 1,000 years castles, gun batteries and forts have been built on the Essex side of the Thames Estuary. Coalhouse Fort, located at East Tilbury, is one of them. Their purpose was to defend the country, especially the river approaches to London, from foreign invaders. However there is little to suggest that they played any useful part in defending the realm in spite of the huge cost of continually rebuilding and maintaining them.

The fortifications proved totally ineffective in June 1667 when a Dutch fleet, under the command of Admiral Michiel de Ruyter, brazenly sailed up the Thames. The Dutch sent raiding parties ashore, virtually unopposed, to Canvey Island and the Isle of Sheppey in Kent. The fleet proceeded to threaten Tilbury but then sailed down the River Medway to sink or burn the cream of the British Navy - the *Royal James*, the *Loyal London*, and the *Royal Oak*. To add further humiliation the Dutch seized the Duke of York's flagship, the *Royal Charles,* and towed it back to Holland. The raid by the Dutch caused panic in London and the King, Charles II, even considered fleeing from the capital.

Tilbury Fort was rebuilt soon after the Dutch incursion. It was another 200 years before Coalhouse Fort was built in its present form on the site of existing gun batteries. An 1860 Royal Commission recommended building a series of coastal *Palmerston* forts, named after the Prime Minister of the day, and Coalhouse Fort was one of them. However it was not completed for another 14 years due to problems with building and several design changes whilst work progressed. The finished fort had 5-foot thick walls. The roofs made of brick and concrete were also protected by granite and iron shields. Charles Gordon (of Khartoum fame) supervised the work during the latter stages.

By the time the fort was ready the rapidly changing technology of gunnery and munitions rendered it obsolete. The casemated heavy-duty structure of Coalhouse Fort restricted the angle of firing the guns or replacing them with newer ones. Practice firings were kept to a minimum as windows could be broken in Tilbury from the shock waves. The life of a gunner was particularly miserable too, due to the deafening noise and choking black smoke in the confines of the casement. Throughout Coalhouse Fort's life guns came and went.

The Fort had never fired a defensive shot in anger until the Second World War when the only operational guns were placed on the roof.

Since 1983 the fort has been leased to the Coalhouse Fort Project. Coalhouse is considered to be one of the finest examples of an armoured casemated fort in the United Kingdom.

**'In action on the roof of the fort
during World War II'**

# THE LOPPER OF LOUGHTON

*Lopping was granted by ancient right,*
*Not to be surrendered without a fight.*

Forest and woodland once covered virtually all of the area from Wanstead to Waltham Abbey and out to Romford. Epping Forest, today, is but a tiny fraction of the once mighty wooded area that existed in Tudor times. Yet even the forest that remains might well have disappeared but for the efforts of one man, Thomas Willingale.

Back in the 16th century the forests were Royal Preserves. As a concession Queen Elizabeth granted a charter giving rights to householders (the commoners) who lived in the forest, to cut wood for fuel and to graze their cattle. However it was strictly forbidden to hunt deer or other game, this was the exclusive privilege of the King or Queen of the day.

Very strict rules were laid down on the practice of cutting wood, which was known as lopping. Lopping was permitted between 11th November and 23rd April (St George's Day) and could only be carried out on Mondays. Only one adult per household could lop. Wood acquired had to be removed on sledges, not wheeled carts and no more than two horses were allowed to draw the sledge. Furthermore it was forbidden to lop branches lower than 7 feet from the ground. Wood obtained was to be burnt as domestic fuel and could not be sold or used for any trade purpose.

As London expanded, more and more forest was cut down for housing, industry and agriculture. At the same time the power of the crown diminished, the word of the monarch was no longer absolute and the upkeep of Royal lands was expensive.

In 1858 the crown sold the rights of the forest, plus 1400 acres of land, to William Whitaker Maitland, the then Lord of the Manor at Loughton. His grandson John inherited the manor and decided to fence off parts of the forest and to ban lopping from his estate. Thomas Willingale had other ideas and jealously guarded his rights handed down from Queen Elizabeth. Meticulously every year at midnight on 11th November, he went into the forest to begin lopping as he firmly believed that if no one started lopping at the appointed hour, the rights would be lost forever.

With the clandestine backing of the local board of works, Maitland decided to prosecute and for 10 years a legal game of cat and mouse went on. One year Maitland even tried to get Thomas Willingale drunk on the eve of the lopping hour in the hope of tricking him into forfeiting his lopping rights.

Willingale died in 1870 but his son, Sam, took up the standard of the loppers. Over the years several fines were imposed on the Willingales. Most of these were not paid and Sam even spent some time in prison for non-payment. The case became a cause célèbre and was viewed as a David and Goliath contest. The Willingales attracted considerable moral, and then financial, support from the City of London and the House of Commons.

There was still lingering outrage at the way much of Hainault Forest had been destroyed 20 years earlier (See page 70, *The Fairlop Frigate*). There was also general alarm at the way huge areas of Epping Forest were being fenced off for the personal gain of a few rich land owners whilst at the same time the public at large were denied access.

Maitland was confronted by a series of legal challenges undertaken by the Corporation of London, which culminated in the Epping Forest Act of 1878. This declared all the enclosures made by land owners in the previous 25 years illegal and henceforth the forest was to become a public open space. The lopping rights ended too but the existing 'loppers' were financially compensated. A sum of money was also put aside to build the Lopping Hall on Loughton High Road.

The forest had been saved and unwittingly the *Lopper of Loughton*, Thomas Willingale, had been the saviour.* Although Epping Forest lies in Essex, the City of London Corporation remains the *Conservator of the Forest*.

* *An oak carved plaque displayed in the Lopping Hall celebrating Thomas Willingale's efforts disappeared during renovations in the 1960s.*

# WILLIAM MORRIS

*His colours reflect the landscape,*
*Of Essex rolling downs.*
*Each thread or blade of grass*
*And stitch of golden corn.*

William Morris was born in 1834, at Elm House in Walthamstow, to prosperous middle class parents. His father's rising fortunes allowed a move from this house, when William was six, to the far grander Woodford Hall. Eight years later, after his father's death, the family moved again to the smaller, but still quite grand, Water House. This, the only one of the three still standing, is today the home of the William Morris Gallery.

Morris left Walthamstow for Oxford University in 1853. It was there that he became lifelong friends with Edward Burne-Jones and later with the Pre-Raephelite Brotherhood, all of whom were influential in his later life. Despite wealth and privileged upbringing, he later embraced the ideas of Karl Marx and became a founding member of the Socialists. He had seen the way that the industrialisation of the nineteenth century had dehumanised production with its emphasis on the 'division of labour'. His answer to what he saw as 'the dull squalor of civilization' was to turn away from mechanisation and seek inspiration from history and nature and draw heavily on the experiences of his Essex childhood.

In the 1830s Walthamstow was little more than a village, bounded by the River Lea and its marshlands to the west, and by green fields and forest. Elm House stood on the rising ground of Clay Hill with views up the Lea valley to Epping Forest two miles away. It was not a 'Grand' house but it stood in its own grounds. With its white panelled hall, wide carved staircase and its garden of flowers, Mulberry bushes and rows of Elm trees it was a place with lots of scope for William's imaginative young mind to develop.

From a young age Morris was interested in romantic tales of chivalry: knights in shining armour, fairies and heroic deeds from history. When the family moved to Woodford Hall he had not only a garden of his own but a large estate and park to roam as well. He had his own pony and even a suit of armour in which he acted out heroic deeds. Riding around the estate and the surrounding Essex countryside he also acquired a love of hunting, shooting and fishing.

Although the family fortunes changed when his father died the move to the smaller Water House made little difference to Morris's life. The house was, and still is, impressive. With its spectacular black and white marble entrance leading to a massive chestnut staircase, it was a watered down version of Woodford Hall.

It was a moated house, the moat at the rear being some forty feet wide with an island in the middle. William and his siblings fished the moat for perch and pike, skated on it in winter and lived out games on their own adventure island. It was an ideal environment in which to indulge fantasies absorbed from his reading of tales of medieval chivalry such as the novels of Walter Scott and the Arthurian legends.

In later life Morris was to say of Epping Forest that as a boy he knew it '*yard by yard from Wanstead to the Theydons, and from Hale End to The Fairlop Oak*'. Through the forest he came to know the trees, the shapes of their leaves and the birds and wildlife that inhabited them. He was familiar with the rivers and marshes and the fish and waterbirds of the Lea and its tributaries.

Morris was fascinated by the ancient earthworks in the forest; Loughton Camp, an early iron age encampment, and Ambresbury Banks, an iron age hill-fort, both reputedly once fortified by King Arthur as a defence against encroaching Saxons. He discovered Queen Elizabeth's Hunting Lodge at Chingford, originally built as a grandstand from which Henry VIII could watch the hunt on Chingford plain. Going inside, his imagination was fired by the faded greenery of the tapestries hanging in the medieval manner and the sheer romanticism of the place. All these experiences and scenes from his early years provided images that would be drawn on again and again in his designs.

In 1853, aged nineteen, William Morris left the family home. After graduating from Oxford he became an artist but design was his real forte. A natural business man, he set up workshops to produce things by hand, with the emphasis on creating beauty while blending usefulness with truth to material, and sound design. His products were an immediate success. His designs of wallpapers, fabrics, furniture and interior decoration made a worldwide impact which is still being felt today.

It was a number of young men in the 1880s, developing their interest in traditional hand crafts and inspired by Morris, who gradually came together to form what became, 'The Arts and Crafts Movement'. William Morris is often associated with the Arts and Crafts Movement; he was not its founder though he was certainly its inspiration.

The **WILLIAM MORRIS GALLERY**, was opened Saturday 21$^{st}$ October 1950 by Prime Minister Clement Attlee and is the only public museum devoted to Morris and his works. The Gallery is located at Walthamstow in the former Water House, set in its own grounds, which now form Lloyd Park.

William Morris is probably best remembered today for his designs of patterned wallpapers and woven fabrics. Examples of these, imitating the flow of water, shapes of birds, the curl of their feathers, the different leaves and their spring and autumn colourings are on display. Some of them no doubt drawn from recollections of his idyllic Essex childhood.

# EARTHQUAKE

*In less than a minute some twelve hundred buildings*
*Were damaged or shattered by waves in the round.*
*Churches lost battlements. Towers and spires,*
*Broken and rent, tumbled down to the ground.*

On the morning of Tuesday 22nd April 1884 at 9.18 precisely, Essex was struck by one of the strongest earthquakes ever to hit the British mainland. It was estimated to have measured 5.1 on the *Richter* scale. The epicentre was between Colchester and Wivenhoe. The quake lasted for about 20 seconds. By the time it was over an enormous amount of property damage had been wrought in the county. The financial cost was huge and as usual the burden fell more heavily on the less well off as poor housing suffered terribly in the destruction.

An eyewitness, Mr. William Ham, gave a dramatic account of the events in Wivenhoe which was later printed in the Essex Telegraph. At the time of the earthquake Mr. Ham was working on a boat moored in the River Colne facing the village. He was quoted as saying *'the first indication I had that anything was amiss was that the vessel rose a foot'*. He went on to report that, as the earthquake shock rolled through the village, every single chimney toppled producing clouds of dust and soot that completely obscured the view.

Although the earthquake lasted only a few seconds, whole villages were wrecked and Colchester was reduced to a state of panic and chaos. In 1884 there was no electric lighting, no telephones, no radio or television and the great majority of people had no idea what an earthquake was. All over the area tiles and chimneys crashed to the ground as roofs collapsed, glass shattered, walls bent and church steeples cracked. The shock was felt as far away as Cheshire and the Isle of Wight although no damage was reported there. Fortunately there were no deaths directly attributable to the earthquake, contrary to some local stories filed at the time. The fact that the earthquake happened in daylight, unlike more recent tremors in this country, may have been a life saver too. There were a number of lucky escapes which included a fisherman on Southend pier who was tossed into the water by the shock and then plucked from the sea by quick thinking colleagues.

There was no shortage of enterprise willing to profit from the disaster. Bearing in mind photography was in its infancy, it is quite remarkable that within days sets of photographs of damaged buildings were being advertised for sale in newspapers. The Great Eastern Railway Company got in on the act too and put on extra trains to bring sightseers to the devastated areas. By the following weekend 2000 visitors were arriving in Colchester on a daily basis by train alone.

Suddenly all sorts of building tradesmen appeared on the scene making extravagant claims about their craftsmanship and honesty. One Colchester man even suggested that a few damaged buildings should be left untouched as a reminder of the earthquake and as a potential tourist attraction!

On a brighter note, a disaster fund was established almost immediately and by the end of July most of the damage inflicted had been repaired. 1884 was a leap year as were the dates of three of the five more recent quakes to strike in this country.

**Panic and Confusion following the Earthquake**

# TIPTREE JAM

*'By their fruits shall ye know them'*
*Strawberries, raspberries, gooseberries and cherries,*
*Currants, damsons, quinces and plums*
*Glorious fruit all there for the picking*
*At Tiptree - the land of superior jams.*

Tiptree Jam has a reputation that has spread beyond Essex, beyond England and Europe to places as far flung as America, Australia, Israel and Hong Kong. It is a reputation inextricably linked to the village of Tiptree in Essex and the Wilkin family. In 1885 Arthur Wilkin's family had already been farming in Tiptree for two hundred years. He was then farming fruit and to get it to market had to take his produce by horse and cart to Kelvedon Station. Increasingly concerned at the damage to his fruit in transit he began making his own preserves. The experiment was so successful that he formed a company under the name 'Britannia'. The venture flourished and before long he decided to use his own name, changing the company to 'Wilkin and Sons Ltd'.

Arthur Wilkin was also the prime mover in establishing the privately owned Kelvedon, Tiptree and Tollesbury light railway line. The line opened in 1904 and was affectionately called the 'Crab and Winkle'. Within 5 years it was carrying 1000 passengers a day plus the finished produce from Wilkin's factory. Unfortunately two World Wars, coupled with the rise of the motor vehicle, saw the railway's rapid decline. Taken over by British Rail the line was closed in 1962.

Arthur Wilkin's company still thrives in Tiptree today with nearly half of all production exported. In the UK Tiptree Jams are a familiar sight in leading department stores and quality food outlets. The demand from London hotels is such that daily deliveries are made to the capital.

The success of this family run firm is the result of generations of Wilkins sticking to the basic philosophy of their founder. The firm has relied upon the people of Tiptree since its beginning. In return it has recognised their contribution and treated them well. Many employees have benefited from profit sharing and the company had pension schemes before the state scheme was set up. Many staff take more than just an employee interest in the business and family involvement is strong. There are numerous examples of succeeding generations of the same family working there, some even living in houses owned by the company.

Some fifty years ago John Wilkin began collecting the paraphernalia of jam making, preserving and Essex Life. The items he brought together now form the basis of the Tiptree Museum which was opened October 1995. Visitors are welcomed and in the well-stocked tearooms the company's products may be sampled.

# GIVE US BACK OUR ESSEX

*Bishops Stortford's Poor Law Union Board*
*Had villages in Essex and Herts to care for.*
*Paying the least they were forced to afford*
*Barely keeping the poorest from death's door.*

Stansted Hall has had many illustrious owners. At the time of the Doomsday Book Robert Gernon owned the estate. It then passed to the Montfichets who gave their name to Stansted Mountfitchet. It was seat of the de Vere family in the fifteenth and sixteenth centuries, apart from twenty years or so when the 12$^{th}$ Earl was executed by Richard III after the battle of Townton. Richard confiscated the estate, only for it to be restored to the family by Henry VII. Since then the incumbents have included Lords Mayor of London and a succession of Members of Parliament until, in the early nineteenth century, it came into the ownership of the Fuller Maitland Family. In 1876 William Fuller-Maitland virtually rebuilt the Hall, creating a mansion suitable to house his priceless art collection. This however was not, as far as Essex is concerned, his greatest achievement.

In 1888 William Fuller-Maitland led a rebellion of Essex villagers against a bureaucratic proposal to change the county boundary to take five Essex villages into Hertfordshire.

The Poor Law Act 1834 had led to the creation of institutions such as the Bishops Stortford Union, which took care of the poor over a wide area. Ever conscious of the need to reduce costs, the board of guardians sought to expand their scope to take in the Essex villages. In collusion with this suggestion the boundary commissioners, bureaucrats to the core who loved straight lines on maps, saw an excuse to straighten out a kink in the boundary line. This would mean that Elsenham, Farnham, Manewdon, Stansted and Ugley would become Hertfordshire villages.

The plan met with fierce opposition and cries of, *We have been Essex Men since Alfred the great,* were heard from the villagers. These outcries were organised into a co-ordinated protest by Joseph Green, a storekeeper backed up by the considerable political weight of Fuller-Maitland. Under this storm of well organised opposition the authorities were obliged to back down and the plan was abandoned.

# KYNOCHTOWN

*Kynochtown was renamed as old patrons had gone,*
*And the new village in the oil refinery was called Coryton.*

The peninsular on which the new village of *Kynochtown* was founded in 1897 was called Shell Haven. There was no connection with the multinational oil giant of today. Shell Haven was so called after the shell bar in one of the creeks by Canvey Island.

*Kynoch and Company Ltd,* a Birmingham based munitions manufacturer, was looking to expand and chose a site on the marshes to build an explosives factory. The second Boer war in South Africa was looming and the extra capacity would help to cope with the expected upsurge in demand for munitions. Coincidentally the Chairman of Kynoch was a brother of the then Colonial Secretary Joseph Chamberlain.

To accommodate the workforce a village was built which originally consisted of forty houses, a school and a shop that also served as a post office. The official naming of *Kynochtown* took place in 1899. By 1903 a working mans club called 'The Institute' had been added. The company also bought land on Canvey Island on which they built the *Kynoch Hotel.* Hotel Guests visiting the factory were rowed across Shell Haven creek. During the Second World War the *Kynoch Hotel* accommodated military personnel, it was demolished in 1960.

Although there was a constant danger from air raids during the First World War the manufacture of explosives continued until 1919. It ceased then, ostensibly due to the risk of flooding, but possibly, with the war over, a downturn in demand may have influenced the decision? The factory closed but the village of *Kynochtown* remained.

Four years later the site was purchased by the Cardiff based Cory Brothers who proposed to construct an oil refinery and associated storage facilities. The village was also renamed *Coryton.* The refinery was built and over the next decade it expanded so much that the village of *Coryton* became completely enclosed within the complex. During the Second World War oil refining stopped and the village was used to house the military.

After the war the Vacuum Oil Company (soon to be Mobil Oil) bought out Cory Brothers and began the construction of another oil refinery. In the meantime civilians had returned to the village.

The new refinery came on stream in January 1953 but was then closed almost immediately by the great flood of that year. During the 1960s, as the industrial site grew, concerns were raised at the wisdom of having housing in the middle of such a potentially dangerous complex.

In the interests of safety all the villagers were gradually re-housed in Corringham and by 1974 the village had been demolished and the name *Kynochtown* almost completely forgotten.

**Visitors transferring to the
Kynocktown Hotel on Canvey Island**

# LONGER THAN A MILE

*Oh Southend Pier longer than a mile!*
*Treading your boards, walking in style.*

Since 1890, when Southend's modern pier was opened, countless thousands have trod its boards. The bracing, mile-and-a-third walk or the thrill of riding the electric trains; the world's longest pier is still, over a hundred years later, a major visitor attraction.

It was in the early nineteenth century that the need for a pier first surfaced. Championed by Alderman William Heygate, a former Lord Mayor of London, the first wooden pier opened in 1830. Initially 600 feet in length, it was unusable at low tide and by 1846 had been extended to 7,000 feet making it the longest pier in Europe. It was bought by the local board, later the council in, 1873.

In the last half of the 19th century the town was changing from being a quiet Essex resort. The London, Tilbury and Southend Railway brought so many visitors from London's East End that they generated the nickname of 'Whitechapel by the Sea'. In an atmosphere of growth and increasing popularity the council decided that the wooden pier should be replaced. James Brunlees designed a new iron structure complete with an all-electric railway and the new pier, which extended as far as the 'Old Pier Head', opened on 24th August 1890.

Steamships increasingly used the pier and by 1908 a 'New Pier Head' complete with upper deck, had been added. Then in 1929 The Prince George Extension brought the pier's length up to 1.34 miles; the longest pleasure pier in the world.

Half a million people enjoyed the pier in 1910. Its popularity increased year on year until and despite being closed during World War Two, it reached its peak in 1949 with seven million visitors recorded. Although numbers have since decreased, they have rarely dropped below the million annually.

The Pier has suffered more than its fair share of disasters. In 1959 the 'Pier Pavilion' was burned down. In its place a ten-pin bowling alley was built, opening in 1962. Then in 1976 another major fire devastated the 'New Pier Head'. Despite this, and the closure of the train service due to track damage, the pier remained open.

Ten years later in the summer of '86, the MV Kings Abbey sliced through the pier between the Old and New Pier Heads causing immense damage.

This was not the first time for such an accident. William Bradley, the first pier light-keeper, and his family lived in a bungalow on the Old Pier Head. In 1889 they were marooned when a vessel crashed through the pier in a similar fashion. They were rehoused ashore and William, who was influential in the formation of the RNLI in Southend, later became an Alderman of the Borough.

In 1995 disaster struck again when the bowling alley was completely destroyed by fire as was 30 meters of track. Nevertheless the pier was reopened within three weeks. The most recent, and hopefully last, calamity to befall the pier was in October 2005. Again it was fire that laid waste the South Station and the Old Pier Head.

The first mile of the pier was reopened to the public on 1st December, and the Pier Head in the following August via a permanent walkway over the damaged area.

Despite all these disasters, plus the ravages of two world wars and being requisitioned by the Navy as HMS Leigh, the pier is still an asset to the town as a major visitor attraction. And, since the Council has pledged that after the recent damage it will be restored, long may it continue.

## SALVATION ARMY COLONY

*The Salvation Army bought the land*
*High above the Old Leigh strand.*
*The unemployed from London towns*
*Were brought by Booth to Hadleigh Downs,*

In his 1890 book 'In Darkest England and the Way Out', General William Booth outlined proposals to help the thousands of destitute unemployed of London. The scheme was mocked and greeted with derision by many in his peer group and Booth anticipated questions from them such as: "Do you think you can create agricultural pioneers out of the scum of Cockneydom"?*

To turn his plan into reality, Booth purchased 800 acres of land overlooking the Thames estuary at Hadleigh, Essex in March 1891, stipulating it should be as far away from pubs as possible. Known locally as 'the badlands', because of its poor farming quality, it became the foundation of the 'Salvation Army Farm Colony'. Eventually the estate comprised 3,200 acres and encompassed the 14th century Castle, farms to the south of Hadleigh Village, Two Tree Island and stretched to the cockle sheds in Leigh. To the north the colony took in much of what is now the Highlands estate and Belfairs Park.

Hadleigh residents did not welcome the plan and were fearful of increased criminal activity. Booth however was determined. Even though a local newspaper accused him of riding roughshod over local feeling and acting as 'Baron of Hadleigh,' local antipathy was gradually overcome. The Salvation Army began to transform the neglected farms. Material was shipped by Thames Barge from the Army's City Colony at Battersea and delivered to a newly constructed dock at Hadleigh Ray. Within three months of purchase nearly 250 'Colonists' were on site busily working under the supervision of Major Wright the Colony's first Governor.

The wide range of farming skills that were taught included care of livestock and poultry, arable crops, orchards and market gardening. A pottery and a brick making works followed and at the peak of operations three separate factories could produce 10 million of bricks annually. The Colonists even built their own railway line which linked the brick works to the dock and an industrial tramway to Leigh-on-Sea mainline rail station.

By the time of its 21st anniversary in 1912 the Army had trained some 7,000 Colonists in skills that could give them a new start. The Colony Farm, as it came to be known, attracted some famous visitors including Cecil Rhodes and J. Rider Haggard who both praised its success.

*\*Gordon Parkhill and Graham Cook 'Hadleigh Salvation Army Farm'.*

Some of the Colonists were even 'contracted' out. A group went to work at Wilkin and Son (Tiptree Jam) picking strawberries. Another detachment was sent to Easton Lodge in Great Dunmow to work on landscaping the gardens where a plaque records the fact to this day.

The two World Wars and the intervening years brought great change. Wounded servicemen were accommodated during the First World War and the military requisitioned much of the land during the Second. Between the wars many colonists emigrated to new lives in Australia, South Africa and Canada, often embarking on ships sailing from Tilbury.

With the introduction of the Welfare State, following the end of the Second World War, the Colony's original aims were no longer relevant although boys on probation and young ex-offenders were still trained there. The last brick works closed in 1956 and for a brief period motorcycle scrambling events took place on the downs.

By the 1960s the farm was being run commercially with profits going to general Salvation Army funds. Then in 1990 a new training centre was launched. Its facilities include a Rare Breeds Centre, the Home Farm Nursery, whose organic fruit and vegetables are sold to the local community, and Tea Rooms with wonderful estuary views. These provide training opportunities, in partnership with local Social Services departments, for people with learning disabilities. There is also a monthly Farmers' Market, run jointly by the training centre and the farm.

Over a century has passed since the inception of the colony. Its size is now more or less the same as the original purchase size. Much of the surrounding area to the south has been incorporated in the Country Park run by Essex County Council.

# THE GILBEY ACCOLADE

*"Sir, in reply to your request, if you ask me,*
*The prettiest village in the East, well let me see,*
*I would say Finchingfield, beyond that I cannot go,*
*Having considered this in depth, it is so".*

As the 19th century came to an end a new leisure pursuit grew up – cycling. Every weekend country lanes became crowded with an ever-growing army of enthusiasts devoted to this new pursuit. As always a popular new hobby produced a number of merchandising opportunities such as cycling spares, clothing and maintenance.

A new newspaper was also born, *'The Rambler'.* First published in 1897, it described itself as *'a penny newspaper devoted to outdoor life'.* *'The Rambler'* ran a feature which encouraged cyclists to explore the countryside and nominate 'the prettiest village in England.' Over 8 weeks the great and the good, or what might be called the celebrities of the day, were invited to write to the newspaper offering their opinion.

Among those to reply to this invitation was one Sir Walter Gilbey of Elsenham, near Stansted*. In a terse letter of 4 lines he wrote:

*"In reply to your letter, if you asked me the finest city in the United Kingdom I should say Edinburgh; and if you asked me the prettiest village in the eastern counties I would say Finchingfield, but beyond this I cannot go".*

Gilbey was the well-known President of the Royal Agricultural Society. His words, published in *The Rambler* on 12th February 1898 and then picked up by the *Essex County Chronicle,* took on a life of their own and became known as 'The Gilbey Accolade'. They were eagerly copied by numerous other publications and travel guides. In the decades to follow almost nothing was printed about Finchingfield without reference to the tag line, in spite of the varying fortunes of the village or the newspaper. *'The Rambler'* went out of business within two years due in part to its small circulation.

At the time of the 'Accolade' Finchingfield was actually in decline. It had lost nearly a third of its population, incidents of polluted water and bad sanitation were reported and a number of houses were considered unfit for habitation and condemned. Nevertheless many painters were inspired by the village and an artist's colony formed. Amongt those attending were Lucien Pissarro and equestrian painter Alfred Munnings. Today Finchingfield has the reputation as the most photographed village in England.

*\* The return distance from Elsenham to Finchingfield is just over 40 miles (64km). That would have been quite an achievement for a man of 67 riding one of the Victorian bone shaker bicycles on the roads of the day, especially if completed over a weekend!*

# TIMELINE

| ESSEX EVENT COMMEMORATED | YEAR | NATIONAL OR INTERNATIONAL EVENT |
|---|---|---|
| Courtaulds gets rights to 'Viscose' | 1904 | *Panama Canal started* |
| Arthur Joscelyne Snr. leases Joscelyne's beach Chalkwell | 1909 | *Louis Bleriot first to fly the English Channel* |
| Morris Dancing Starts in Thaxted | 1911 | *Hiram Bingham finds Machu Picchu* |
| Death of Captain Oates | 1912 | *Titanic sinks on maiden voyage* |
| Zeppelin L33 crashes at Lt Wigborough | 1916 | *Battle of the Somme* |
| Kynocktown becomes Coryton | 1919 | *IRA is formed* |
| Loftus Arkwright disappears | 1919 | *League of Nations founded in Paris* |
| First Public Entertainment Broadcast | 1920 | *Prohibition comes into effect in USA* |
| Bertram the Clown opens in Clacton | 1922 | *Stalin becomes Soviet Leader* |
| Crittall's Model Village created | 1925 | *Logie Baird transmits TV pictures* |
| Borley Rectory Investigated | 1928 | *Fleming discovers Penicillin* |
| Happy Harry assaulted in Southend | 1929 | *Debut of Popeye in comic strip* |
| Two Churches in Willingale combine | 1929 | *Wall Street Crash* |
| Plotlanders expansion in Dunton | 1930 | *First Football World Cup* |
| Ford begins production in Dagenham | 1931 | *National Government formed in UK* |
| Bata Shoe Factory opens East Tilbury | 1933 | *Hitler appointed German Chancellor* |
| Galleywood Racecourse closed | 1935 | *Alcoholics Anonymous formed in NY* |
| | 1939 | *Start of World War II* |
| Leigh boats rescue troops from Dunkirk | 1940 | *Winston Churchill becomes PM* |
| RAF Bradwell Bay opens | 1942 | *Irving Berlin writes White Christmas* |
| Stansted Airport opens as USAF base | 1943 | *Battle of Stalingrad ends* |
| Mulberry Harbour Section sinks in Thames Estuary | 1944 | *'D Day' Landings in Normandy* |
| | 1945 | *World War II Ends* |
| The Great Surge: Essex Floods | 1953 | *Hilary and Tensing climb Mt Everest* |
| Bradwell Nuclear Power Station opens | 1962 | *Uganda becomes independent* |
| Last train from Saffron Walden | 1964 | *BBC2 starts broadcasting* |
| Radio Caroline begins broadcasting | 1964 | *Harold Wilson becomes PM* |
| GLC formed, Essex borders changed | 1965 | *Rhodesia declares UDI* |
| Radio Caroline silenced by storms | 1966 | *England Wins World Cup* |
| Weely Rock Festival | 1971 | *Decimal currency introduced in UK* |
| Chelmer Navigation closed to freight | 1972 | *Bloody Sunday in Northern Ireland* |
| Southend Pier Head destroyed by fire | 1976 | *First Concorde passenger flight* |
| Space Shuttle Enterprise lands at Stansted | 1983 | *Margaret Thatcher wins 2nd Election* |
| New Terminal opened at Stansted | 1991 | *First Gulf War, Iraq invades Kuwait* |
| Nuclear Bunker Decommissioned | 1992 | *'Black Wednesday' UK leaves ERM* |
| Elizabeth Fry new face of £5.00 note | 1992 | *English FA Premier League formed* |
| Brightlingsea Live Animal export protests | 1995 | *OJ Simpson verdict: 'Not guilty'* |
| Death of Sir Alf Ramsay | 1999 | *Welsh Assembly opens in Cardiff* |
| Bradwell Nuclear Power Station Closes | 2002 | *EURO notes and coins introduced.* |

# FAMILY COURTAULD

*George Courtauld - descendant of a French refugee*
*Opened a silk mill in the town of Braintree.*
*After nine good years he retired knowing well*
*That the mill would be safe with son Samuel.*

George Courtauld, the great grandson of a French Huguenot refugee, opened his own silk mill in Braintree in 1809. This was the beginning of a long and fruitful association between Braintree and the Courtauld family. George brought his radical Unitarian principles into the business and it flourished. One of the difficulties he faced as business improved was in recruiting labour. Ideally silk spinning required young nimble fingers, preferably girls aged 10 to 13. Having exhausted the supply of young children locally, Courtauld started taking girls from 'well run' workhouses in London. The workhouse contracted to pay him £5 for each child taken and a further £5 after the first year. He insisted that each child came with 'a complete change of common clothing' and was bound apprentice until the age of 21. In return he promised that his mill would 'prove a nursery of respectable young women fitted for any of the humbler walks of life'.

George Courtauld was a believer in social reform. In 1813 some of his apprentice girls ran away, claiming that their supervisor had badly beaten them. Courtauld, while disclaiming any liability, immediately dismissed the supervisor and set his four daughters the task of caring for the apprentices. They arranged a system of marks to monitor the work and behaviour of the girls. Taking their responsibilities seriously, they were setting the tone for the future, in terms of the whole family being involved in the company. The firm was regarded locally as a good employer. In 1818 George decided to retire to live in America where he died in 1823. His son Samuel took over the mill.

Under Samuel the mill thrived and he expanded with mills at Halstead and Bocking. An innovator, he introduced steam power to the Bocking mill and by 1835 Halstead boasted over two hundred power looms. By the mid-century the Courtauld mills employed above two thousand people.

Although it was Samuel that put the company on the road to success it was very much a family concern. Brothers, sisters, sons, daughters, and cousins all played their part. Samuel's wife Ellen employed a nurse and organised a crèche for working mothers, probably the first company in the country to do so. Mothers would drop their children off at 6a.m. and pick them up at 6p.m. and they would be given 'boiled rice and treacle for their dinner'. For the employees a Workmen's Institute and evening classes were set up.

The firm started to become the world-wide organisation it is today when, in 1904, Samuel's son, also Samuel, acquired the rights to the 'Viscose system'.

This led to the discovery of 'Rayon' and many other 'man-made' materials revolutionising the clothing industry as well as products as diverse as tyres, power transmission belts, furnishing fabrics and even cigarette filters.

If the family were rich they were also generous and evidence of this may still be seen in Braintree still. As early as 1862 George (the second) Courtauld bought the land and built Manor Street School, currently the Braintree District Museum, and in 1871 his wife founded the Cottage Hospital in Broad Road, now a private house. They also funded the Braintree and Bocking Institute to foster study and learning. The Public Gardens are today much as they were in 1888 when Sydney and Sarah Courtauld gave them to the town. The celebrations at this event were said to rival those for the Queen's Jubilee the previous year. Sydney's son, William Julien, continued the tradition by giving the town the William Julien Courtauld Hospital, the Fountain in the Town Square and the Town Hall. This stands on what was the cattle market and in earlier more gruesome times was where, on March 28th 1555, a Protestant martyr, William Pygot, was burnt at the stake. It is now the tourist information centre.

Perhaps the best known, outside Braintree, philanthropy of the Courtaulds came from Samuel IV, company chairman until 1946. Together with Viscount Lee of Farnham and Sir Robert Witt, he was responsible for the foundation of 'The Courtauld Institute'. The original aims of the institute were to provide a forum for an academic study of art history. These aims, with the co-operation of London University, are still being achieved today. Samuel was an avid collector particularly of French impressionist art and his collection formed the basis of much that can be seen at the Courtauld gallery in London today. As a very wealthy man Samuel Courtauld was continuing the family tradition of always putting something back into society.

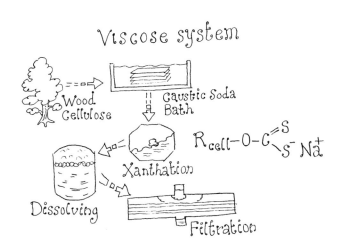

## JOSCELYNE'S BEACH CHALKWELL

*"Nine Pound". She cried "Nine Pound!*
*To lease a stretch of shingle!"*

We may all do something risky once in our lives when dealing with the family finances but Arthur Joscelyne senior's little business venture in 1909 may take some beating. One Saturday in March he rushed home from the *Smack Inn* in Old Leigh. A little worse for wear, demanding lunch be put on hold, he went straight to the mantelpiece and scooped the contents out of the china jug which held all the family savings. His wife was dumfounded and asked what was going on, to which he replied,

*"Sorry love can't stop, I've just seen a man in a pub and I'm going to buy a beach",* and without further ado he was gone.

Later that day Ellen Elizabeth, his wife, discovered what had become of the nine pounds savings. She was not too pleased to put it mildly. Arthur Joscelyne had purchased from the Southend and Tilbury Railway Company a four-month, June – September, lease on a beach at Chalkwell. It was triangular in shape and measured just 200 yards in length and, when the tide was in, about 50 yards depth at its widest point.

The Chalkwell of 1909 had no station or easy way to the seafront. The railway line that ran from Leigh to Southend-on-Sea completely cut off access to the sea. On the sea side of the line a rough cinder path ran from Leigh Old Town, parallel to the track, atop crude stone sea defences. The building of the sea defences had been somewhat haphazard and as a consequence large chunks of rock littered the beach, which were a hazard to bathers and boats alike.

In spite of all the obstacles, both financial and physical, by the end of the first season Arthur Joscelyne had installed a large shed on the beach. This served as a focal point and the creation of a fine business was in the making. Ellen had now accepted the situation and wholeheartedly endorsed the project. The next year the lease was renewed. Gradually the beach was cleared of stones and rocks. Changing tents were put up and a small fleet of boats were made available for hire and trips. Fishing was popular and the sale of bait and rods was lucrative. The business grew and even flourished during the First World War. A severe blow came in 1917 when Arthur senior died suddenly of a strangulated hernia. Ellen took the helm and Arthur junior, at the age of 14, stepped into his father's shoes.

Every year throughout the 20s and 30s, including the general strike and the years of economic depression, Joscelyne's Beach was open for the summer.

However it was gradually becoming more and more difficult to maintain its privacy as Westcliff-on-Sea and Southend became established as seaside resorts.

Apart from that, and the odd storm or exceptional tide that swept away the changing tents and boats, business continued as normal until the Second World War.

At the outbreak of war all the Essex beaches were closed. When the war ended Ellen, now aged seventy, resumed the business but it was short lived. In 1948 the government nationalised the Railways and thus ended the leasing arrangement. Private beaches were also considered out of character in the post war Britain. Ellen died shortly afterwards. The area is still known to locals as Joscelyne's Beach and the path that runs from Leigh to Chalkwell station is still known as the cinder path although the cinders, have long since gone along with the steam trains that created them.

# THAXTED

*In twelve-eighty-seven one Richard de Taxte*
*Was known as a hafter in the village of Thaxted.*

After the Norman invasion of 1066 the Saxon settlement of Thaxted, which had grown up since Roman times, became one of the 'spoils of war' in common with many Essex lands. As such The Manor of Thaxted was granted by William the Conqueror to one of his supporters and relatives, Gilbert Earl of Clare. Unlike his kinsmen de Vere, Montfitchet or de Mandeville, Gilbert did not build himself a great castle and the Manor buildings disappeared during the fourteenth century. The Manorial system was in decline somewhat then and the Peasant's Revolt of 1381 may have contributed to this.

In the late thirteenth century the power of the Trade Guilds was on the increase. Thaxted had become home to a thriving cutlery industry and it is known that in 1287 Richard de Taxte, working as a hafter or maker of handles, was a member of the Cultlers Guild. Their importance to the town was demonstrated by the building of their impressive Guildhall, a little over a hundred years later, between 1390 and 1400. The cutlery industry disappeared during the sixteenth century and the Guildhall became an administrative centre for the town. It was used as a school for many years and today is still used by the Parish Council for meetings and as an exhibition space.

The other most significant building that has survived is the Church of St John the Baptist, St Mary and St Lawrence. Begun in about 1340, in the reign of Edward III and completed 170 years later in the reign of Henry VIII, its 181 feet tall spire dominates the town today as it has done for six hundred years.

In the early 1900s Conrad Le Despenser Noel became vicar, appointed to the living by The Countess of Warwick of nearby Easton Lodge. The Countess was well known for her radical left wing political views and, like her, the Reverend Noel also acquired a reputation as a radical socialist. In memory of the fourteenth century peasant leader John Ball, he set up a *'Chapel of John Ball, priest and martyr, 1381'*. He also flew a red flag over the church throughout the general strike of 1926, as well as on every May Day.

Famous for his flower processions and country dancing, in 1911 Conrad Noel and his wife, Miriam, encouraged the formation of a 'Morris' club. Thus began the internationally famous tradition of the Thaxted Morris, making the town a national centre for Morris dancing. In 1934, after a meeting in Thaxted, 'The Morris Ring' was formed. For many years clubs from all over England have gathered in front of the Guildhall soon after Whitsun, to perform their dances in spectacular displays with two hundred or more dancers.

Every year on the Saturday before the 24<sup>th</sup> June, (John the Baptist's Patron Saint's day), the Morris is performed. It is also performed on Easter Monday, the Bank Holidays in May and August, and on Boxing Day.

Sir John Betjeman once said, *"There is no town in north Essex – and few in England – to equal in beauty, compactness and juxtaposition of medieval and Georgian architecture, the town of Thaxted."* The Church, built on a cathedral plan, has often been referred to as 'The Cathedral of Essex'. Its interior is no less impressive and has fine acoustical qualities. It was these that the composer Gustav Holst appreciated when he visited in 1913.

A year later Holst came to live in a thatched cottage in Monk Street where he wrote his 'Planets' suite. In 1916, he organised the first Whitsuntide Festival in Thaxted. Also a socialist, he became a friend of Conrad Noel for whom he wrote 'Christian Socialist music' for his 'people's processions'. Holst reinvigorated the musical tradition of Thaxted with these early festivals. One of his pupils, Jack Puterill, was ordained and became curate, then vicar, of Thaxted. A talented musician himself he encouraged many great performances in the church. Thaxted has been host to among others, Sir Adrian Boult, Norman Del Mar and Yehudi Menuhin, conducting some of the great orchestras of the country.

The musical tradition continues to this day. In 1980 Michael Snow, building on the town's growing reputation, began the Thaxted Festival. For a number of weeks each summer, this festival provides a series of musical events of outstanding quality and national importance. The setting both visually and acoustically is unique in what is probably one of the finest parish churches anywhere.

# I May Be Some Time.

*"I'm just going outside and may be some time."*
*Simple words, profoundly spoken to chime*

Visitors entering the village of Gestingthorpe may puzzle over the face on the village sign. The face is that of the village's most famous son, Captain Laurence Oates, who crawled out of his tent and into a blizzard with the famous parting words, "I am just going outside and may be some time". This action, in temperatures of minus 40 degrees, taken to maybe give his colleagues a better chance of survival, is the stuff of legend. His final remark as he went to certain death has become a byword for the ultimate in self-sacrifice.

Laurence Edward Grace Oates was born on March 17th 1880 to William and Caroline Oates. He joined his elder sister Lilian and was followed by brother Bryan and sister Violet. William Oates had inherited considerable wealth and on Laurence's birth certificate described his profession as 'Gentleman'. He was also a notable 19th century explorer and with his young family moved around quite a lot both in England and abroad. In June 1891, when Laurence was eleven, the family moved into Gestingthorpe Hall. The vast park surrounding the house, with its fruit trees, pond, tennis courts, swathes of grassland and stables, was perfect for the children to explore and enjoy. It was here that Laurence's passion for horses began.

At fourteen it was decided that young Oates needed a formal education. He was duly despatched to Eton in the hope that he would progress to Oxford. This was not to be, academically his time at Eton was not a success and in his second year he became seriously ill after contracting pneumonia. Recovering at home, he never returned to Eton. Later he decided upon a military career, his love of horses leading to enlistment, in 1900, in a Cavalry regiment, the Inniskillen Dragoon Guards.

As a Second Lieutenant Oates was posted to fight in the Boer War. On one particular foray, when in charge of a scouting party, he was shot, the bullet smashing his thighbone. In great pain and under fire he resisted repeated calls to surrender and was eventually rescued. For his bravery he was awarded the Victoria Cross. He returned to Gestingthorpe to recuperate.

On recovery, left with a pronounced limp, he returned to duty serving in Egypt where he was promoted to Captain and made Adjutant of the Inniskillen's. This was followed with spells in Ireland and India but he was becoming disillusioned with military life. On hearing of Scott's planned expedition to the South Pole he bought his way out of the army at a personal cost of £1,000 – some £50,000 in today's terms.

Scott planned to use Siberian ponies to haul the expedition sledges and Oates joined the team primarily as the expert on horses.

Some would say he should never have gone on the expedition. A bullet wound in the Boer War had left him with one leg two inches shorter than the other. This, and the fact that he was a cavalry officer and the horses, bought without his knowledge, were in Oates' words the "greatest lot of crocks I have ever seen", made him not ideally suited to crossing 1,800 miles of Antarctica on foot.

Though frequently clashing with Scott, and feeling at times isolated as the only army man on what was essentially a naval expedition, Oates was disciplined and a team player. He managed the horses for the first four hundred miles but they were not up to the task. Oates was envious of the Norwegian Roald Amundsen, who reached the pole a month before them, and his good sense to use dogs. Their surviving horses were shot and left where they fell in the frozen waste. A proposal to use the meat for food was rejected by Scott. Now it was Scott's men who had the backbreaking task of hauling the heavy sledges.

It was on the return journey that Oates realised he had become a burden and was holding them back. He was suffering from severe frostbite and gangrene in his feet, which he had kept from his colleagues. Probably as a side effect of scurvy, his old Boer War bullet wound in his thigh had opened up and become an open sore. He was virtually starving and rational thought must have been difficult. Whether a combination of pain, cold and hunger plus a real concern for his colleagues' survival was the reason for Oates suicide, or that he chose the time of his death knowing he would not survive, it is impossible to know.

That his sacrifice was in vain is a matter of record. His colleagues Scott, Bowers and Wilson may well have been beyond realistic chance of survival when Oates went out. In fact Scott, maybe sensing that the end was nigh, wrote his first letter of farewell on the day Oates died. The letter included the phrase, "…we have been to the Pole and we shall die like gentlemen". They struggled on but all perished some eleven miles from the food depot that could have meant salvation.

It is charitable to believe Oates had his comrades in mind when he crept out to his death on his birthday, 17th March 1912. That the expedition ended as it did in no way detracts from his heroic action.

# L33

*Having dropped bombs on London without inhibition*
*The Zeppelin turned for home to complete its mission*

September 1916: London was under threat from the latest German 'Super Airships'. Zeppelins were an awesome sight, 680 feet long cigar shaped balloons containing two million cubic feet of gas. Their aluminium frame structure, covered by a varnish impregnated skin and weighing fifty tons, could carry a load of sixty bombs.

On the night of the 23rd of September, one of them, designated L33, had bombed London causing much death and destruction. On turning for home across Essex it was hit by anti-aircraft fire and damaged by night fighters from RAF Hainault. Having just managed to limp across the coast, L33's Captain Alois Böcker, on his first mission, despite jettisoning guns* and equipment into the sea, realised that he would not make it home. He turned his ship back towards Mersea. The Zeppelin eventually made a forced landing near New Hall Farm in Little Wigborough in the small hours of the morning.

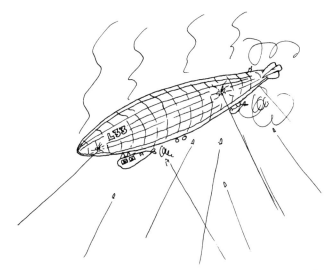

Böcker's priority was to destroy the airship. Before setting fire to it, the captain knocked on the doors of New Hall Cottages to warn the residents. The terrified the occupants did not open their doors. With the airship burning fiercely the Germans marched off in the direction of Colchester with no option but to surrender.

Special Constable Nicholas who was cycling to investigate the blaze met them on the road. He dismounted and, recognising Böcker's German accent, accompanied them to Peldon Post Office where they were formally arrested by PC 354 Charles Smith. Peldon did not have a Police Station, and the Post Mistress declared, 'They can't stay here.' PC Smith promptly telephoned the military base on Mersea. He then marched the whole group to rendezvous with a military detachment, and formally handed them over, thus ending the war for Böcker and his crew.

The Chief Constable, on hearing the news of his prompt action, promoted PC Smith to the rank of Sergeant. Until he died, at the age of 94, he was known by all as 'Zepp' Smith.

At nearby Great Wigborough, Mrs Clarke, of Abbotts Hall, gave birth to a daughter at about the same time as the Zeppelin was burning. The doctor attending her, Doctor Stanley, recorded in his diary that he had suggested that the baby might be christened, 'Zeppelina'. He did not record whether his advice was taken.

L33 was one of two Zeppelins to raid London that night. The other, L32, did not reach London and dropped its bombs on Purfleet. It was shot down over Burstead. There were no survivors from the crew of 22.

*A jettisoned machine gun fell on land owned by Wilkin and Son (Tiptree Jam). It was promptly recovered and put on display in their factory. The Army, on hearing of this, arrived a few days later to confiscate the weapon. However a photograph of the gun can be seen in the Jam Museum.*

# MISSING PERSON FROM HARLOW

*Old Loftus Arkwright was never the same*
*When his son went missing - of the same name.*
*He went from fair Harlow we do not know where,*
*'Disappeared' on his family tree - if you look for him there.*

The name of Arkwright, inextricably woven into Britain's industrial revolution, is usually associated with the *'dark satanic mills'* of northern England. Less well known may be the long association that, for over a hundred years, descendants of Sir Richard Arkwright, the inventor of the 'Waterframe' spinning machine and a very wealthy figure in the early industrial revolution, had a with the Harlow area of Essex. This connection ceased with the fifth generation of Arkwrights providing an unsolved mystery, – What happened to Loftus Arkwright?

The Harlow connection began with Sir Richard Arkwright's son, also Richard. Successful like his father, he became one of the richest men in England. His son Joseph, an ordained clergyman, married Anne, a member of the wealthy Wigram family of Walthamstow.

Anne's father Sir Robert Wigram suggested to Richard Arkwright that he buy Mark Hall estate, to provide a home for Joseph and Anne, and install Joseph as the vicar of St Mary the Virgin (Now St Mary-at-Latton). Joseph duly became Squire of Latton and Vicar of St Mary's. As well as developing a passion for foxhunting, he expanded the estate which he had inherited on his father's death.

Loftus Wigram was the seventh of Joseph's twelve children and shared his father's love of the hunt. He was given the management of Little Parndon Manor, which Joseph had acquired by 1850. A talented farmer, he was the only son to remain at Latton. On Joseph's death in 1864 he inherited the whole estate including Mark Hall.

Loftus Wigram built himself a new house, Parndon Hall, which still stands today, and serves as an education centre for the local Hospital NHS Trust. He became a magistrate and was Master of Foxhounds until breaking his back in a hunting accident. Later, he still followed the hunt but was driven in a light open carriage. He died suddenly in 1899, leaving all the estates to his only son Loftus Joseph.

Loftus Joseph was very much in the Arkwright tradition. He went to Eton and Cambridge and was passionate about hunting. Like his father, he was Master of Foxhounds until a serious accident put an end to his riding days too. In 1894 he married Julia Caldwell, the daughter of his rich American tenant of Mark Hall, and in 1895 their first son, just plain Loftus, was born. Twin brothers Godfrey and John came along in 1901.

The Arkwright estates continued to grow under Loftus Joseph. By 1930 he had acquired the manors of Netteswell, Passmores and Canons in Great Parndon and other properties from Harlow to Roydon under the umbrella of the 'Mark Hall Estates Company'. His wife had left him in 1919 and in his latter years Loftus Joseph became increasingly eccentric and reclusive. He was rarely seen in public and died in 1950. He is buried in St Mary's churchyard, Little Parndon.

Traditionally Loftus, the eldest son, would inherit but he had rebelled against generations of Arkwright tradition. Unlike his father, or his twin brothers, he had no interest in hunting, the church, the armed forces or even expanding the Arkwright property empire. At the age of twenty-five, having left the family home to work in a garage, he simply disappeared. This was in 1919, the year of his parent's separation and eventual divorce. Did he change his name and just drop out of circulation, meet with an accident or even emigrate? Whatever happened he has not been heard of since, although there have been rumours that he lived the life of a hermit in Africa.

Since Loftus' brother John had died at sea in 1942 his twin Godfrey inherited Parndon Hall. He left Parndon after three years and died within six months. The Arkwright Estates were purchased for the Harlow New Town development. The only known direct link to the Arkwrights of Harlow is Godfrey's son John who held the patronage of St Mary-at-Latton and St Mary's Little Parndon but he moved abroad some years ago. He in turn had a son, Loftus Edward born in 1961. His whereabouts also remain unknown.

The Arkwright name is remembered today in the housing area, 'Arkwrights', in Netteswell. The walled garden of Mark Hall is open to the public but the Hall, visited by Queen Elizabeth I (see page 47, Harbingers at Harlow) and once home to Newman Gilbey, of 'Gilbey's Gin' fame, has long been demolished.

# Radio 2MT (TwoEmmaToc)

*The inventor of radio and wireless,*
*His genius unrecognised in Rome,*
*Came to England seeking success*
*And made Chelmsford his technical home.*

Guglielmo Marconi was born in Bologna in 1874 to an Italian father and an Irish mother. At the age of twenty he was experimenting in communicating intelligence, without the use of connecting wires. Within two years he had invented the first practical radio-signalling system able to transmit signals over a few kilometres distance. He offered his invention to the ministry of posts and telegraphs in Rome but they were not interested. Disappointed, he left Italy for England with his mother in February 1896, to be met by his cousin Henry Jameson Davis.

After being introduced to William Preece, Engineer in Chief at the Post Office, Marconi patented his system and formed the 'Wireless Telegraph and Signal Company Ltd'. Continuing his experiments on the roof of the Post Office in London, in 1899 he established communication across the English Channel. In 1901 he successfully communicated between Poldhu in Cornwall and St John's, Newfoundland.

Marconi's company began manufacturing in a former silk mill in Hall Street, Chelmsford. The 'radio factory' flourished and in 1912 a new factory was built in New Street to cope with demand.

Eager to explore public entertainment broadcasting, Marconi gained ministerial approval to make an experimental broadcast. This took the form of a concert, sponsored by the Daily Mail, broadcast from a specially built studio at New Street. The concert, featuring the famous soprano Dame Nellie Melba, was widely publicised. It was transmitted on 15th June 1920 at seven o'clock London time. It was a great success, heard clearly wherever there was equipment to receive it.

Based on this success the Post Office gave permission for regular entertainment broadcasts from Writtle using the call sign Two Emma Toc (2MT). Regular transmission began in February 1922. Later a second station, using the call sign 2LO, began broadcasting from the top of London's Marconi House, Aldwych in May of the same year. On the basis of this success the new British Broadcasting Company was formed and public service broadcasting as we know it was born.

Some fourteen years later in 1936, using an aerial and transmitters designed and made in the New Street factory, the BBC began the first scheduled television service in the world from Alexandra Palace in the River Lea valley. (see page 164, - Down the River Lea)

Guglielmo Marconi died on 20 July 1937. Thousands of mourners lined the streets at his funeral in Rome and transmitters around the world observed a two minutes silence. Though he lived much of his life in England, he never lost touch with his family home. He is buried there in the grounds of the Villa Griffone at Pontecchio near Bologna.

Today a bronze statue by Steven Hicklin commemorates Marconi's place in the history of Chelmsford. Unveiled on 'International Marconi Day', 26th April 2008, it stands in the 'Marconi Plaza' adjacent to the Civic and Cramphorn theatres.

**Dame Nellie Melba**

# BERTRAM THE CLOWN

*At three in the afternoon Clown Bertram performed and impressed
the boss and for 18 years the pier never made a loss.*

In 1922 Albert Edward Harvey turned up unannounced at the Clacton
Pier office of Barney Kingsman and patiently waited to see him. Kingsman had
just acquired Clacton Pier and a fleet of ageing passenger vessels, the *'Belles'*,
from the liquidators.

Eventually Harvey was shown in where he was gruffly asked, "What do
you want boy? Can't you see I'm busy"?

Harvey said he was a children's entertainer using the name 'Bertram' and
was looking for work.

'That's all I need' said Kingsman, thinking aloud. He immediately
summoned his foreman and barked, "This boy claims to be a children's
entertainer so give him a week's trial, then sling him out".

Kingsman returned to contemplating the long list of pier repairs
outstanding and pondered on how much they would cost. The following
afternoon, working in his office, he was disturbed by a huge din coming from
outside. Kingsman stormed out to complain only to find an amazing sight. An
extract from an interview concerning the pier in a 1934 edition of the magazine
'Tit Bits', sums up the scene:

*'At the end of the pier a thousand people were standing, and scores of children
sitting on a bit of carpet, and they were shrieking with laughter, while a young man,
aided by a couple of children from the audience, played a burlesque drama…. It was
a riot.'*

That was the beginning of Clown Bertram. The week's trial was to last for 18 years! The pier had originally opened in 1877 during the great period of Victorian Pier Building.

Its original purpose was to serve as a landing stage for trips for London city dwellers wanting to escape the pollution and grime of the metropolis. The passenger steamers did good business until the arrival of the railways. Then trippers could get to, and return from, Clacton more quickly with the added advantage of not being sea-sick en-route.

Kingsman therefore took the decision that the future of the pier was destined to be in entertainment – especially in the light of the continuing success of Clown Bertram.

Kingsman invested almost every penny he had, and could raise, in the pier. He need not have worried. Clown Bertram kept pulling in the crowds.

At first he performed in the open, then in a specially built theatre accommodating 500 at the pier head. However the audience soon outgrew that too. The old pier pavilion was remodelled, renamed as the *Jollity* and its capacity increased to 1000. This too was frequently full to capacity. Often many adults and children would queue for hours so desperate were they to get in.

Clown Bertram was the best loved performer ever to appear on Clacton Pier and some famous celebrities to be, such as Jimmy Hanley and Warren Mitchell (Alf Garnett), appeared with Bertram as child amateur performers. The show had an unbroken run from 1922 to 1939 and unusually for many 'stars' Bertram went out on a high. The outbreak of World War II brought entertainment on the pier to an abrupt end. Clacton was closed for the duration of the war except for local residents and the military. Bertram never appeared there again. Albert Edward Harvey died at the age of sixty five, happy in the knowledge that he had brought joy to thousands of children.

# CRITTALL'S NEW JERUSALEM

*Workers could be hired but with nowhere to house them,*
*What was a keen socialist like Francis Crittall to do?*

In October 1849 Francis Berrington Crittall arrived in Braintree and opened an ironmongery business at 27 High Street (now Bank Street). It was here, above the shop in 1860 his second son Francis Henry was born. On completing his schooling Francis Henry was sent to Birmingham to work for a bedstead maker where he met and married his wife Laura. After the death of his father in 1879 his elder brother Richard ran the business for a while but had no interest in it. In 1883 Francis Henry returned to Braintree to take over and Richard left to live in London. Francis Henry was an ambitious and inventive engineer and this small shop, under his control, grew into the global Crittall manufacturing business. It survived for over a hundred years with the Crittall family at the helm. Francis Henry had two sons who were both involved in the business. Valentine George, born in 1884, also became the Labour MP for Maldon and was later created Baron Braintree. The second son Walter Francis was born in 1887 and he became the artistic and technical director of the company. Walter was given the nickname 'Pink' as a child and throughout the company was always known as 'Mr Pink'.

The company's breakthrough came in 1900 with the invention of standardised metal window frames. These were to revolutionise the building industry and create huge demand.

During the First World War the company diversified into armaments and military equipment. Employing around 2,000 men at this time, the company was still expanding and was desperately short of housing to accommodate its ever growing work force. Francis Crittall also had a nickname and was known (throughout the factory) affectionately as 'The Guv'nor'. A keen socialist, he held the view that a happy and contented workforce was a productive one. With this in mind he set to solve the accommodation problem. First he toyed with, and then discarded, the idea of building a housing estate near Braintree. Encouraged by his sons who were also admirers of the 'Garden City' movement, he decided to emulate Titus Salt and George Cadbury and their model villages of Saltaire and Bournville.

On November 3$^{rd}$ 1925 Crittall's purchased for £7,500 the 200 acre Boars Tye Farms near Silver End on which to build their garden village. There was enough land for a population of seven to eight thousand people. Self-sufficiency was the byword for the project and strengthened the philosophy of, 'a happy workforce is a good workforce'.

Drainage, water and electricity supplies, all were to be unique to the village. It would contain churches, a school, a cinema, a hotel and its own department store selling food from a company owned farm. It even had its own bus service.

The houses, many designed by 'Mr Pink' who was influenced by the German 'Bauhaus' modernistic style, each had their own garden. They had hot and cold running water which was not found in many homes at that time. The hot water came from the factory's excess capacity. They were built on tree lined avenues, with plenty of public space in the form of gardens and recreational areas. A new factory, commissioned as the house building started, supplied electricity to the residents from its own generators.

The 'Silver End Development Company' was set up to build the village. One of the directors, Captain Reiss, brought his experience as a member of the board of 'Welwyn Garden City' to the project. The style of the village was 'Modern' and one of the few examples seen in Essex. The completion of the Silver End project was overseen by Valentine George. When the village was fully functioning his parents took up residence in 'The Manors', a large detached house where they lived until Francis' death in 1934.

Valentine George was an ardent believer in the welfare state and introduced his principles into the company. He employed people with disabilities at the same rates of pay as anybody else. The conditions of employment were in advance of most and the good relations with the workforce were evidenced by the fact that throughout the general strike in 1926 normal production continued undisturbed. In 1931, in recognition of his efforts in promoting the workers welfare, he was given a knighthood and, in 1947, elevated to the peerage as Baron Braintree. He was also made a director of the Bank of England and had responsibility for transferring the printing of banknotes to the new factory in Debden, Essex.

At its peak Crittall's employed 5,000 people. The company prided itself in being progressive and it was the first major company in Britain to abolish Saturday working, by introducing, in 1926 a five day, 45 hour week. Witham and Braintree benefited immensely from the Crittall patronage. The company's permanent sports ground was opened in 1923 on Cressing Road. It covered 17 acres and had some of the finest facilities in the country.

In 1968 the Crittall business was bought by Slater Walker Securities and the family connection ended when Walter 'Mr Pink' Crittall retired in 1974. Although the company produced their 50 millionth steel windows in 1978, and today Witham is home to Crittall's International business, the late 20th century saw the company's decline from its former success. The housing at Silver End was acquired by Witham Council and designated a conservation area. Many of the houses are now owned privately. Nevertheless Silver End remains a fine example of the social experimentation of the nineteenth century embodying the ideas of the Garden City Movement.

# HAUNTED HOUSE

*Borley Rectory sadly is no more.*
*A lamp was knocked over on a pile of books*
*And the days, and nights, of yore*
*Were gone (or were they?) for the resident spooks.*

Borley Church has stood, close to the Suffolk border with commanding views of the River Stour valley, from Saxon times. In 1863, the Reverend Henry Dawson Ellis Bull built a new rectory close to the church to house his growing family. The large brick, castle-like construction, was a forbidding building, surrounded by tall trees and subject to peculiar acoustic effects from the wind. It had attics, cellars, several staircases and eleven bedrooms and was a warren of a building. Seventy five years later the Rectory was burnt down by the owner, William Gregson, in a deliberate act of arson and as a bogus insurance scam, according to insurance investigators.

In the intervening years, largely due to the *Daily Mirror* and the psychic investigator Harry Price, the house gained the reputation of being the most haunted house in England. Even today ghost hunters regularly hold weekend vigils in the grounds of Borley Church. At Halloween and mid-summer, larger gatherings of spirit seekers descend upon Borley and the police need to keep a strong presence to maintain order.

Local legend has it that the Rectory was built on the site of a 13th century monastery from which a Monk eloped with a Nun from nearby Bures Convent, escaping in a coach and horses. Soon captured they were brought back and punished. The Monk was hanged and the Nun bricked up alive in the Convent. Although there never was a monastery at Borley there have been many alleged sightings of the couple and a phantom coach and horses. Another tale was of a black clad Nun who walked the garden. This phantom was claimed to have been seen by four of Bull's daughters, in daylight, in July 1900.

When H. D. E. Bull died in 1892 his son Harry took over as Rector. He married at the age of 48, much to the disgust of his unmarried sisters who made life unbearable for his young wife. They even accused her of poisoning him when he died in 1927. Harry Bull was eccentric in many ways and firmly believed in the ghost of the phantom Nun. He is alleged to have threatened his family that he would return from the grave. These characteristics are all woven into the legends of Borley.

In 1928 the new incumbent, the Rev. Eric Smith and his wife Mabel, arrived. They were regaled with stories and rumours of strange happenings; footsteps, lights being turned on or off, doorbells ringing and keys disappearing. Whether they were taken in or not is not known but it was Eric Smith that contacted the *Daily Mirror* who sent a reporter to investigate, together with Harry Price. They reported objects being thrown across rooms, and the reporter claimed to have seen the Nun. The Smiths moved out in 1929 but not before Mabel Smith had made detailed notes for her book, *Murder at The Parsonage,* which was never published.

Lionel Foyster, a cousin of the Bulls, took over as Rector in 1930 and moved into the rectory with his wife Marianne, twenty-one years his junior. It was during their five year stay that the tales of hauntings really grew. The Foysters, also intended to publish a book (though this never happened), in which two thousand psychic happenings were recorded. There is suspicion that the 'happenings' were created by Marianne with Lionel's connivance. Harry Price, who was involved with them throughout, had his doubts yet he still described the Foyster's tenure as "The most extraordinary and best documented case of haunting in the annals of psychical research".

The Foysters left Borley Rectory in 1935. Harry Price then leased the building for a year. During this time he recorded objects moving and the sounds of footsteps but nothing comparable to Marianne's earlier claims. The results of his investigations as well as many of the Foyster's 'happenings' are recorded in his two books, *'The Most Haunted House in England'* and *'The End of Borley Rectory.'*

On leaving Borley Marianne confined Lionel, who was by then a sick old man, to the attic of their new house in Suffolk, at times passing him off as her father. She is reputed to have had a string of adulterous affairs at Borley but went even further in Suffolk when she bigamously married a travelling salesman. After Lionel's death Marianne married an American Serviceman and moved to the USA in 1946, where she lived until her death in 1992.

As for the Rectory, it burnt down in 1939 when William Gregson, its last owner, overturned an oil lamp amongst piles of books, though this version was disputed by the insurers. Maybe the ghosts perished in the fire?

There are those who believe in ghosts whatever the evidence may indicate and for them Borley will no doubt always hold fascination. On the other hand tales of adultery, bigamy, jealously, poisoning and possible murder are subjects which, probably founded in fact, are equally gripping.

# HAPPY HARRY

*The crowds come and go, as the morning turns to evening.*
*It's time to go, but let us sing once more:*
*'I'm H. A. P. P. Y. I'm H. A. P. P. Y.*
*I'm H. A. P. I'm H. A. P.*
*I'm H. A. P. P. Y.*

Happy Harry was a familiar figure to the thousands of people who visited Southend's seafront between 1910 and 1966. An old style evangelist preacher, he took his chance on what was known as Southend's 'Speaker's Corner'. There was competition from other speakers representing the Salvation Army, the Exclusive Brethren, the Elim Church and many others, plus the political movements. As Harry put it, *"Marine Parade was like a lunatic asylum at weekends".* It was his happy revivalist singing and preaching that drew the big crowds. He attracted dozens, and on occasion hundreds, of people to listen spellbound, always on the same spot, by the rain shelter on Marine Parade just to the west of Pleasant Road.

Happy Harry's real name was the Reverend George Wood. He had spent a year at Bible College before being ordained as a minister in the Pioneer Pentecostal Church in 1909. Two years later he was called to preach in Southend. It was through his efforts that the first Pentecostal Church in Southend was opened in Clarence Road in 1919. Rev Wood preached there for eighteen months and was paid £12 per month. Apart from this, he relied upon the generosity of his audience on the seafront for his sole income. He lived in Oakleigh Park Drive in Leigh-on-Sea with his wife and son and, in the absence of a steady income life cannot have been easy.

A preacher first and foremost, Harry was also a natural entertainer and the crowds loved him. He was not a big man, he would stand on a folding chair, or sometimes just on the pavement, and sing out in a voice that belied his smallish frame.

*'There's something more than gold my friend, There's something more than gold*
*To know your sins are all forgiven, Is something more than gold.'*

This would soon attract an audience. It would be followed with a story from the Gospel delivered in Harry's inimitable style, more singing, then finish with what, for many, became his theme song:-

*'It's rolling in, it's rolling in.*
*The sea of love is rolling in.*
*I believe that I receive*
*The sea of love that's rolling in.' etc.,*

This chorus was a signal for his audience to roll pennies and halfpennies towards Harry. On one occasion a man was heard to shout "Here y'are Harry, here's a penny, give us a ha'p'ny change." And Harry did. It was this sort of action, done with a smile, that endeared him to many as much as his preaching. However there were some people that made his life a misery and at times their abuse got out of hand.

Stories abound amongst those that remember Happy Harry of the trials and tribulations that he had to bear. When people rolled coins to him, occasionally young children would run in and pinch them before Harry could pick them up, and there was always heckling. These things he could meet with a smile. Hooligan nastiness appeared at times when young men would heat up pennies with cigarette lighters to burn Harry's fingers when he picked them up; once they tied newspaper to his coat tail and set fire to it.

Sometimes things were so bad that police were called to break up demonstrators. He was once lifted bodily by two men who would have thrown him in the sea had it not been for the intervention of some of his audience. In another incident he took a blow to the face which smashed his glasses, leading to the loss of sight in one eye: His attacker was fined two pounds! It is said that some of the most hurtful abuse he received was from conservative Christian elements that hated his Pentecostal movement.

None of this deterred Harry from his preaching. His devotion to religion led to his separation from his wife (although they were together again in 1960) and estrangement from his son. He said of this, *"I regret hurting them but I am happy, I have seen thousands of converts to the Pentecostal Church"*.

In 1938 Happy Harry was admitted to Runwell Mental Hospital as it was known. He didn't stay there long. On his 'release' he stood for election as an independent candidate for Southend Borough Council. He put on his election address that *'I am the only candidate who has been certified sane'*.

During World War Two Harry worked for the War Office as a messenger until 1954. He later worked as a commissionaire on the door of Lyons Corner House in London. Never in good health, he still preached regularly after work and at weekends, not only in Southend but in London and as far as Bedfordshire.

In 1966, his health failing, Harry moved to an old folk's home in Streatham, south London. In 1972, 'The Hot Gospelling Rev. George Wood,' was brought to Southend by the 'Evening Echo' to relive his memories, 'of crowds of people singing and praying and his own voice thundering out urging them to a better way of life'. It was his last visit to the town. 'Happy Harry' died in 1974. He is remembered by a plaque erected by the Southend Society, situated on the sea wall approximately two hundred metres west of Pleasant Road, a few steps away from Harry's pitch by the shelter.

# Two Sisters, Two Churches

*From birth they wanted everything they touched.*
*Each fighting for anything the other one clutched.*

Willingale is a small village situated between Ongar and Chelmsford with a population of about 450. It has two churches, *Willingale Spain* and *Willingale Doe.* It is unusual for such a small community to have two same faith churches and it is extremely rare for both churches to be built on the same plot of land next door to each other!

Researching back in time for hundreds of years to find out why locations for certain buildings were chosen has always proved a challenge. Records may not have been kept in the first place or they may have disappeared through neglect, accident or deliberate action. Without documentary evidence it is often impossible to distinguish between the 'fact' and legend.

One of the explanations for Willingale's churches' side by side existence was that each served to accommodate the spiritual needs of two rival sisters. This supposition is mentioned in all area guide books and can be traced back to the Victorians. With the passage of time more detail has come to light, or alternatively the story has been embellished.

The two sisters in question were of Saxon descent called Beornia and Synnove. A year apart in age, they were daughters of Rheda and Aeschere, a noble Knight. From the time the sisters were first able to communicate the two siblings bickered. Initially they argued over playthings or food but then it was clothes, their tutor or the attention received from their parents. As they developed into young women they fought for the affections of Tristram, son of Hew Rhyddol a Norman landowner. Relations between the Saxons and the Normans were fractious at the best of times. To spite her sister Synnove provoked a fierce argument between Tristram and her father which got out of hand and resulted in both men's deaths. The sisters could not even find solace in their shared grief so their mother Rheda financed the building of a second church to enable them to pray separately for redemption.

Plausible though this legend is, the archaeological evidence shows that the churches were built approximately 200 years apart. The first church, *Willingale Spain,* was built after the Norman Conquest under the patronage of Hervey D'Espania. Also known as D'Ispania he came over with William the Conqueror and was responsible for Spain's Hall near Finchingfield.

In about 1320 the D'Ou family arrived in Willingale. They were wool merchants. Wool and cloth were expanding industries in early 14th century Essex and probably the biggest employers after agriculture. As the local population increased, the church was not large enough to accommodate the worshippers.

Rather than pull it down and build a larger one the D'Ou family built asecond church, *Willingale Doe,* beside *Willingale Spain* and on land already consecrated. A new parish was created which gave the village a second priest.

In 1929 the two churches were united again. However *Willingale Spain* fell into disuse and became a virtual ruin. It was restored in the 1950s by the *Friends of Friendless Churches* although it still has no electricity. Today both churches fall within the parish of Willingale with Shellow and Berners Roding, all of them sharing the same priest.

It is possible that the two sisters lived in the 1320s when the second church was built. In that case the argument that resulted in the deaths of a suitor and the father of the sisters could have happened. *Willingale Doe* could have been built to keep the grieving sisters apart. However the Saxon connection is only relevant during the eleventh century, the time of the building of the first church, when there was a real divide between the victorious Normans and the defeated Saxons. By the fourteenth century this had disappeared and a new national identity was taking shape - Englishness.

# 'HISTORY IS BUNK'

*'History is Bunk', so Henry Ford said,*
*It means nothing we don't want tradition.*

*"History is more or less bunk".* So said Henry Ford in an interview with Charles Wheeler for the Chicago Tribune on May 25th, 1916. Yet history will no doubt show that Ford made a significant contribution to the development of the small Essex town of Dagenham.

Ford had been producing the 'Model T' since 1913 at Trafford Park, Manchester. After the 'Great War' demand was such that to meet it a new factory was needed. The nation-wide search for a site finally settled on Dagenham riverside where Samuel Williams owned much of the land. His Company's development of Dagenham dock, providing shipping access together with good road and rail links, made it an ideal site. In 1924 Ford bought five hundred acres from Samuel Williams and the 'Ford Dagenham Car Plant' was under way.

In 1928 Henry Ford decided to come and inspect the new project. He and his wife, Clara, set sail for England, travelling incognito as Mr and Mrs Robinson, maybe to avoid publicity since, though highly successful, Henry Ford was not universally popular. While here he met King George V and Queen Mary and the leading politicians of the day.

Henry, impressed with the new project, appointed Sir Percival Perry to re-launch 'Ford Britain' as the hub of his new European organisation. In December 1929 Ford Motor Company Limited (UK) was floated and work on the new Dagenham factory started.

When production began in 1931, two thousand workers and their families were brought on special trains from Manchester to their new homes in Dagenham. Many more were hired locally. On October the first 1931, the Managing Director, Roland Hill, drove the first vehicle off the assembly line, a Fordson AA truck.

During the forties, due to the importance of Ford's war effort, workers needed permission to leave, even to join the forces. By 1951, despite post war shortages, the new 'Consul and Zephyr' range came into production and Ford was employing upwards of forty thousand people. By 1996 ten million vehicles had been built at Dagenham since production started in 1931.

The names of some of the cars - Anglia, Cortina, Capri, Sierra and Mondeo were all famous in their day and the name Ford is inextricably linked with the history of modern Dagenham.

Car production ceased in Dagenham on 20th February 2002 - the last vehicle off the line was a Ford Fiesta. Powered by wind turbines the plant now contains Ford's designated centre of excellence for the design and manufacture of diesel engines. The finished engines are exported to plants all over the world.

**The First off the Line**

**The Last off the Line**

# PLOTLANDERS

*From London to Dunton they came, a trickle then a rush*
*Seeking respite from the overcrowded, noisy, smoky city crush.*
*Whole families wanting a weekend retreat or holiday home*
*Came to the countryside where it was clean and free to roam.*

Although, in late Victorian times, London was a dirty, grimy city and heavily polluted it was nevertheless expanding and confident. A new class was emerging. This was not the land owning gentry and certainly not the desperate city poor that existed on the margins of society. This new class consisted of bank workers, skilled artisans, civil servants, merchants, teachers and managers. In recent times they might be called the middle class. They had a measure of job security, a roof over their heads and above all some disposable income.

At the same time conditions in the countryside were anything but rosy. Since 1870 farming had been depressed. Farms were going bankrupt with the land virtually unsaleable. Food was increasingly imported from abroad, and much of the land was deemed unsuitable for farming. A report to a Royal Commission in 1898 described a large portion of Essex farming land ' *not fit for purpose*'. Subsequently recommendations were made that the land be sold off, not as whole farms but in small units or plots. Almost immediately the property developers of the day realised the financial potential and the 'plotlands' scheme was born.

Areas of land, roughly from Laindon to Dunton and north to Billericay were offered for sale. The average size of the plot was 20ft X 160ft and was offered at £5.00 a plot. An acre could be bought for £30.00 but there were few takers. Plots were marketed to Londoners as '*land in the countryside - in fresh clean air*'. They were also described as '*the ideal weekend or holiday retreat for hard working town folk*'. To begin with take up was slow but it grew steadily, and although interrupted by the First World War, reached a frenzied peak in the early 1930s. The salesmen used all sorts of persuasive inducements in what were known as the '*Champagne sales*'. Prospective buyers were offered free or discounted return rail trips from London, lunches, champagne of course and numerous other incentives in order to make a sale.

The new owners took to their acquisitions with gusto. At weekends the Laindon countryside was packed with Londoners engaged in the new fad of DIY. All types of temporary buildings and shacks sprang up with quaint names such as *Daisy Dene, Cosy Nook and Lilliville*. Lorries, vans and even old railway carriages were converted. Building materials and furniture arrived by any means available, even motorcycle. On Sunday nights the platform at Laindon station was often packed eight deep, for its whole length, with weekenders waiting to catch the last train back to London.

The sudden influx of people living on the plotlands brought problems as at first there was no mains water, no drainage and, most important, no sewerage facilities. Water was laid on to properties closest to the station and a series of standpipes were erected.

The local council, Billericay, became somewhat alarmed, not only about the provision of water but at the state of some of the homes that were erected. Several prosecutions were issued over the haphazard construction of some dwellings.

During the Second World War many people used their plotland homes as refuges from the London Blitz. This was no guarantee of safety since enemy aircraft used the Thames as a guide to London. They could be shot down and crash nearby. Damaged planes could, and did, jettison their bombs and unspent ammunition over the area.

After World War II, much of the capital lay in ruins. There was a desperate need to re-house many Londoners. One of the solutions to this was to create the New Town of Basildon. Some plotlanders came back and some new Londoners took up vacated sites, but recreational tastes were changing. Caravan parks were springing up and holiday camps were booming. Most plotland sites, however, were cleared by the New Town Corporation to satisfy the huge demand for housing. The clearing continued until 1980.

Today a substantial green area of plotland remains as the Langdon Nature Reserve run by The Essex Wildlife Trust. Close to the entrance to the park is *The Havens,* an 'original' plotland dwelling that serves as a museum.

# WHERE IS ZLIN?

*People flocked to Tilbury on hearing the news*
*Thomas Bata needed people to make his shoes.*

Zlin lies 1000 miles from Essex, in the south-eastern corner of the Czech Republic, close to Vienna and Budapest. A large wall map displayed in the Bata Resource Centre in East Tilbury shows Zlin at the centre of the world. It was the birthplace of Thomas Bata who created the Bata Shoe Company. Bata founded his company in 1894 and his dream was make cheap affordable shoes for everyone. He also wanted shoes to be made in modern clean factories by a contented workforce that enjoyed good pay and welfare conditions. Back in Victorian times owning a good pair of shoes was a luxury and once acquired they were expected to last a lifetime. Working conditions were grim, with virtually no health or safely regulations at work and little sickness care or pension provision.

Bata was not a utopian idealist. He was a businessman who believed that a happy worker was a productive one. This philosophy had been proven in the Zlin factory. To further his ambition to be the *'shoemaker to the world'* he chose East Tilbury, Essex as the site for his factory in the UK. It would not, be just a factory but a self-sufficient community on the original Zlin model. Work started in 1932 under the direction of Czech architects Vladimir Karfik and Frantizek Gahura. Everything would be built as seen in a normal town – an hotel, a cinema, restaurants, a dance hall, sports facilities, a garage, and shops including a shoe shop. The community would even have its own newspaper *'The Bata Record'.* Everything, however, was owned by Bata.

Production began in 1933 but Thomas Bata never lived to see shoes coming off the production line in East Tilbury. He was killed in a plane crash a year earlier. His half brother, Dr. Jan Bata, took over the helm at the company.

The arrival of the Bata Company in Essex aroused many misgivings. Like most countries, Britain was suffering from economic depression and mass unemployment following the Wall Street Crash. 'Foreigners' coming to Britain to set up factories and telling the British how to run them caused alarm in some quarters. The press carried several reports reflecting these sentiments. Doubts were expressed about the new welding techniques used in the structure of the factory. There was criticism too of the fact that there would be Czech foremen supervising locals. A number of letters were also published about boys (the Bata Boys), some as young as 14, being sent off to Czechoslovakia to train for up to three years. In those days foreign travel was almost unknown except for the colonial service, the military or the privileged few.

It was the fear of the new and the different that caused most of these concerns. Gradually Bata overcame resistance to their presence and their way of operating, despite a prolonged strike about union recognition in 1937. Yet through all the difficulties in the first few years people travelled from all over the county, often on foot or bicycle, to seek work with Bata.

The company benefits for workers were previously unknown, certainly in East Tilbury. Housing was provided for families and young unmarried workers were often accommodated in the company hotel or hostels. High standards had to be maintained and discipline was rigid. Even the state of the gardens was regularly checked.

On arrival workers were greeted with rousing music at the factory gates to welcome them in. However, lateness or slacking on the job was not tolerated. On dismissal not only the job would go but the house too. The Bata's management did their level best to create a cult feeling of loyalty to the company.

Towards the end of the 1930s the dark clouds of the Second World War were looming and those senior members of the Bata family still in Czechoslovakia fled to England, the USA or Canada. The war gave a boost to production and the factory turned out thousands of military boots. After the war the Bata Family remained in exile as the new communist masters in Eastern Europe nationalised all the factories. Thomas Bata junior did not return to his homeland until the end of the Soviet era in 1989. For a time Bata was one of Britain's biggest exporters and had more than 3,000 people working on site.

The machine-age logic that created both Zlin and East Tilbury were the seeds of their demise. Continuing technical innovation required fewer people. General industrial malaise in Britain in the 1970s and stiff competition from Europe, and then the Far East, hastened the end. The last shoes were made in East Tilbury in 2006. Since 1993 the factory and estate housing provided by the company for its employees have been part of a designated conservation area. A bronze statue of Thomas Bata stands outside the front of the old factory building.

# LITTLE SHIPS OF LEIGH

*'Defender, Endeavour, Letitia*
*Reliant, Renown and Resolute :-*
*Were the little ships sent from Leigh*
*They had to join 800 more*
*To sail to Dunkirk's distant shore*
*And change a course of history.'*

May 1940. Hitler's armies had marched through Holland and Belgium and were sweeping across France. The British Expeditionary Force (BEF) and the French forces retreated and were cut off. A German spearhead reached the sea, leaving the allied forces trapped in a small area of coast around Dunkirk. On the 26th May a contingency plan to evacuate the troops, code named *'Operation Dynamo',* was swiftly put into action by the admiralty. On May 30th, from Southend pier, requisitioned by the Navy as 'HMS Leigh', requests were made for volunteer crews and their shallow draft vessels to help in the exercise.

The response from the fishermen of Leigh was immediate. Arthur Dench was the first to report with his boat 'Letitia'. He was quickly joined by five other Leigh cockle boats, the 'Defender, Endeavour, Reliance, Renown and Resolute', and their crews. These six boats, under the overall control of Sub-Lieutenant Solomon RN, left Southend Pier at 11:00 am on the 31st May bound for Dunkirk. Although coming under attack from German bombers, they arrived at close to seven in the evening and promptly set about ferrying stranded troops from the beach to the larger ships anchored in deeper waters.

The Leigh Bawleys with their broad beam and flattish bottoms, designed to cope with the Thames estuary sandbanks, were ideally suited for this work. Although only thirty feet in length and ten feet wide, between them they rescued many thousands of soldiers. In fact the total rescued by the armada of small boats commandeered for this operation was in excess of three hundred thousand.

In the early hours of June 1st the Leigh men started for home. The Renown had developed engine trouble and at 1:15 am hailed the Letitia who took her in tow. Thirty-five minutes later, as Arthur Dench recalls in Shiela Pitt-Stanley's book 'Legends of Leigh', *"A terrible explosion took place, the Renown had hit a mine and a hail of wood splinters came down on our deck. In the pitch dark we could do nothing except pull in the tow-rope, which was just as we had passed it out to the Renown three-quarters of an hour before. But not a sign of the Renown."* The rest of the Leigh boats continued to Ramsgate then on to Leigh where they were met by their families waiting at the waterside.

Arthur Dench said of the Renown's crew, *"They knew nothing of war. They went to save, not to fight.....It was a small tragedy in the great disaster of those days of war yet great in the hearts of Leigh people."*

On June 4th a letter of appreciation from Naval Control to Sidney Ford of Leigh read, *"The ready willingness with which seamen from every walk of life came forward to assist their brother seamen of the Royal Navy will not be forgotten."*

In May 1968 these events were commemorated at St Clements Church by a plaque and flags being dedicated in the Chapel of the Resurrection. In 1972, in the churchyard, a memorial was erected to the Fishermen of Leigh, and specifically Frank and Leslie Osborne, Harry Noakes and Harold Graham Porter, the crew of the Renown.

The Endeavour is the only surviving Leigh boat of those that went to Dunkirk. Registered with the 'Association of Dunkirk Little Ships' it is now back in Leigh after extensive restoration.

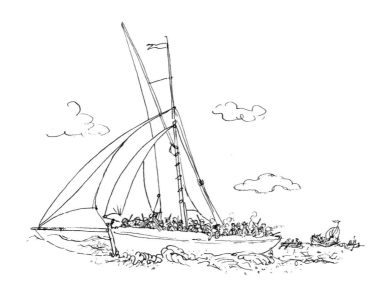

# STRIKING BACK

*After the dark days of forty one,*
*There was a job that needed to be done.*
*No longer just defending the land*
*Taking the fight to the enemy was planned.*

On the Dengie peninsular not far from Maldon, the old Magnox towers over the banks of the River Blackwater. This was Britain's first commercial nuclear power station and is built on the site of an old RAF airfield - Bradwell Bay. The airfield became operational in April 1942 when the Second World War was in its third year. Slowly the tide of battle was turning in favour of the allied cause. The threat of invasion to the British Isles had receded and there was an increasing determination to take the fight to the enemy.

The first arrivals at Bradwell were Canadians manning a squadron of twin-engine Boston aircraft painted in matt black. These aircraft were used as intruders for night operations over occupied Europe. Soon after, there followed a British mosquito squadron employed to attack specific enemy targets in France. As the war progressed many more squadrons came and went, or were rotated through, as the allies advanced after D Day. During the airfield's life, apart from the British and Canadians, New Zealanders, Australians and Czechs were based there.

A whole variety of ancillary missions were undertaken such as pathfinding, bomber escort and troop carrier support, the latter especially for the D-Day landings, and the airborne landings at Arnhem in Holland. Of vital importance was the airfield's role in Air Sea Rescue. Returning aircraft were often forced to ditch in the sea. Sometimes they just ran out of fuel before reaching land. Homecoming Halifax and Lancaster bombers would also use Bradwell Bay as an emergency landing site because of its close proximity to the coast. The last operation from Bradwell was in April 1945 and the airfield closed completely in December that year.

An impressive cast iron replica 'Mosquito' is the centrepiece of the memorial which stands on the corner of the original site. One hundred and twentyone aircrew were lost flying from Bradwell Bay. A stone displays the names of the missing flyers with the legend:-

*'who in answer to the call of duty*
*left the airfield to fly into the blue forever'.*

# MULBERRY

*Trips around the Mulberry and tales of yesteryear*
*That sailor men have told to me whilst holding back a tear.*

Just over one mile from Thorpe Bay's shore, in the Thames on the West Knock sandbank, a 2,500 ton concrete Phoenix caisson lays partially sunk in the mud. It is a section of the Mulberry Harbour destined for use after the D-Day landings in World War Two and has remained there for over 40 years.

*Operation Overlord*, the invasion of Europe by 250,000 allied soldiers, took place on the 6th June 1944. It was an unprecedented logistical challenge. It was assumed that all the major French ports would be unusable which meant the allies needed to take their own harbours with them to support the landings and to re-supply the troops once ashore.

Most of the caissons were built in and around docks on the River Thames. Parts of the East India, Royal, Tilbury and Surrey docks were drained so the work could be carried out. Each concrete caisson was hollow and if made watertight would float, although it is difficult to imagine concrete caissons weighing up to 5,000 tons bobbing about on the high seas. The plan was to tow them to the site of the proposed harbour location on the Normandy coast and sink them in position. They would then serve as supports for the landing bridges.

The section sitting on the West Knock sandbank was not made on the Thames. It was one of six built in Goole dry docks on the River Humber by Henry Boot and Company. Classed as C1s these were the smallest of the caissons. One of them, while being moved south, sprang a leak off the River Crouch. It was towed into the Thames Estuary to await inspection and repair but in a squall it broke free from its anchor and ran aground. The concrete shell was punctured, flooding it. At low tide it settled and broke in two which made it virtually impossible to recover. Building the caissons was a huge task and undertaken in great secrecy. An apprentice. Frank Agar, who worked on the project for four months, commented that the workers had no idea what they were building. Some speculated they were concrete barges! Apart from the 500 people employed on building the six made in Goole another 6,000 worked on them in Essex. The name *Mulberry* was not significant, simply a code word for harbour and one of numerous code words originating during the war. The concrete caissons were coded *Phoenix*.

A fleet of ocean-going tugs towed them to Normandy after D-Day. Two harbours were built, the first just off Arromanches supporting the British and Canadian sector and the second at Omaha Beach for the Americans. Within days of the landings the port for the British and Canadian sectors was working to full capacity. The second Mulberry at Omaha started well but was then wrecked by a freak storm two weeks later. The *Phoenix* caisson at Thorpe Bay was one of over two hundred built.

# DOWN THE RIVER LEA

*Legend has it that when the Danes*
*Sailed up the river and landed,*
*King Alfred and a few of his Thanes*
*Blocked its flow and left them stranded.*

The River Lea rises at Leagrave Marsh in Luton, Bedfordshire, 52 miles (83kms) from where it joins the Thames at Bow. In the 9th century the river formed the natural boundary of the Kingdom of the East Saxons. It remained the dividing line between Essex and London until local government reorganisation in the mid 1960s, which extended London's boundary into Essex as far as Hornchurch.

As London grew and prospered many of its industries were moved from the centre to make way for grand housing and places of business. Tanners, slaughterhouses and workshops producing too much noise, effluent or smell were the first to be pushed out of the fashionable City and Westminster areas. The Lea valley to the east was seen as an ideal place for industrial relocation. The waste products could be dumped in the river and washed out to sea. This practice made the River Lea, from Hackney to Bow, one of the most polluted rivers in the country. It was still the case in the late 1950s. White Post Lane, which crosses the river at Hackney Wick, was dubbed '*Smelly Lane*' by locals due to odours created by nearby factories or the stench coming from the river.

In the last two hundred years the Lea Valley has been a hive of industrial activity. Almost everything connected to the modern industrial world has at some time been manufactured in the Lea valley including ships, railway locomotives, vehicle engines, telecommunications equipment, copying machines, matches and armaments. The river has always served as a transport conduit to move goods out and raw materials in.

In 1804 William Congreve manufactured rockets in a factory on a site now occupied by the Bromley by Bow gas works. These rockets were probably the first tactical surface to surface missiles built. They were used, with limited success, in the Peninsular War. Upstream the famous Lee Enfield rifle was made at the Royal Small Arms Factory at Enfield lock. This rifle was the standard issue in the British army for 60 years although 'Lee' was the designer's name and nothing to do with the river!

After the Second World War demand for household electrical goods grew exponentially. Lea valley companies such MK Electric, Belling, Thorne and Ferguson met the demand and became household names. Innovations in valves, transistors and the use of plastics in electronics resulted from pioneering research in the Lea Valley.

It was from Alexandra Palace, on the western banks of the river, that the world's first public television broadcast took place at 3pm on the 2nd November 1936.

The post war boom was relatively short lived. By the new millennium all the heavy industry and most of the manufacturing base had gone. It had been relocated well outside London or disappeared overseas. Expansion of commerce and corporate activity within London, which created Lea Valley industry in the first place, was equally to blame for its demise. A huge demand for additional housing pushed up land values. Old inefficient factories closed as the owners sold the land for development, moving their businesses to cheaper locations or just taking the money.

Some large areas of land still remained derelict in spite of the pressures of housing due to years of serious contamination.

The Lea is a river of contrasts. Upstream the river feeds a dozen reservoirs, which in turn supply much of the capital's drinking water. As for the derelict land salvation is coming in the form of the London Olympic Games due in 2012 with the centrepiece Olympic stadium due to be built at Marshgate Lane. A large proportion of the budget for the games has been set aside for cleaning up the polluted areas, enabling the Lea Valley to undergo yet another revival.

# ARMAGEDDON

*Into the bowels of the earth*
*Went the six hundred, the chosen few.*

On the A128, between Brentwood and Ongar, prominent signs can be seen with directions to the *'Secret'* Nuclear Bunker. It might be more accurate if the signs read; *'This way to the Nuclear Bunker that is no longer secret'.* Once one of the most hush-hush places in the land, the bunker has become one of the more unusual tourist attractions in Essex.

In 1952, officials from the War Office turned up at the Kelvedon Hatch farm of Jim Parrish with a compulsory purchase order for 25 acres of his land. This was the beginning of the Nuclear Bunker. Almost immediately public access to the site was banned, local roads were closed and the designated area fenced off and patrolled by armed guards.

The first contractor arrived to excavate a huge hole. This was followed by a succession of builders all working under the cloak of the *Official Secrets Act.* Secrecy was paramount, each group completed their allocated task and left. None of them knew what anyone else was doing or what the final objective of their labour was. Work commenced on 1st October 1952 and working non-stop throughout the winter months, much of it in the dark, the bunker was completed by the following March. The only visible evidence was a quite ordinary looking bungalow.

Underneath this innocent façade, however, going down 100 feet, was a three-story bunker encased by 10 feet thick reinforced concrete walls. The entrance was shielded by steel blast proof doors weighing one and half tons each. It was hoped the bunker and its inhabitants could survive the force of a close proximity nuclear explosion.

The originally purpose of the bunker was to serve as a ROTOR station. ROTOR was a government code word used to describe the upgrading of air defences at the inception of the Cold War. The Kelvendon Hatch location was one of a number built on the East Coast of the British Isles. The *Marconi* Company installed in each bunker the most up to date radar and communications equipment available.

As the Cold War intensified, and the Soviet Union acquired nuclear weapons, the British Government's response was twofold. Firstly British nuclear weapons were developed and tested, and then planning began in earnest as to how the nation would cope with a nuclear war and its aftermath.

The role of the bunker was changed to that of Regional Government Headquarters, with the code name RGHQ 5.1, and £10 million was spent on modifications to it. In the event of the unthinkable, nuclear attack, the bunker would serve as the control centre for London and the surrounding area.

Within it 600 key personnel would be lodged. They would include top civil servants, cabinet ministers and even the Prime Minister of the day. The bunker was fully self-sufficient, with its own power supply as well as water and food for three months. There was also a 2,500-line telephone exchange and a BBC radio studio that could broadcast to the nation's survivors.

A great deal of thought had gone into the nuclear doomsday scenario. A series of civil defence films were made to explain how the population at large should prepare for nuclear war. Most of these were never shown on the grounds that they might cause panic. If the bomb dropped, scientists in the bunker would monitor fallout and radiation levels and advise on the risks. It was assumed millions of people would die - but millions would live. However it was supposed many of the living would have a short life expectancy due to severe burns, radiation sickness and lack of medical attention or even starvation. There was no provision to take family members into the bunker. The unit was to be protected by guards outside who would keep unwanted intruders out, and just as important, keep the key personnel in. Just how the guards were to survive is unclear!

In 1989 the Berlin Wall came down and two years later the Soviet Union began to break up. The Cold War was effectively over. The Government decided the bunker was no longer needed. The £3 million annual running costs may have speeded this decision. In December 1994 ownership of the land, including the bunker, reverted to the Parrish family. They have preserved the bunker as a historical reminder of what may have been.

During its 'operational' lifetime when nuclear *Armageddon* was a distinct possibility there were just two ways to get in or out of the bunker - the entrance tunnel or the emergency stairs at the rear. With the Cold War over and since becoming a tourist 'attraction' a third exit has been added - on the grounds of health and safety!

# THE GREAT SURGE

*With night, the surge increased the further south it travelled.*
*On reaching Essex one by one the sea defences unravelled.*

At 9.46am on Saturday 31st January 1953 the Princess Victoria, a British Railways car ferry on a routine crossing between Stranraer and Larne in Northern Ireland, sent the following message:-

*"Hove-to off mouth of Loch Ryan. Vessel not under command.*
*Urgent assistance required".*

At 10:32 an SOS was transmitted. The order to abandon ship followed. All the women and children were put in lifeboats. Shortly after the vessel was overwhelmed and sank. The lifeboat capsized in the mountainous seas and none of the occupants on board survived. In all 130 passengers and crew perished.

Four hundred miles further south on Canvey Island in Essex, news of the disaster was slow to filter through. Televisions were a novelty and the telephone a luxury. Although the sinking was the top story on radio, details were sketchy. The 24-hour breaking news we know today was then unknown. Those who had heard about the disaster, whilst shocked and saddened, carried on as normal. That same Saturday brought storm force winds and rough seas but nothing out of the ordinary. After all it was mid-winter. The 31st January was to be a great occasion for Canvey Island with the opening of the War Memorial Hall on the High Street by the Deputy Lieutenant of Essex. A brass plaque to the 57 islanders killed in the Second World War was to be unveiled. It was a grand event to celebrate the successful fund-raising effort that had made the hall possible.

As the Canvey Islanders prepared for the celebrations, unbeknown to them a huge depression was moving around Scotland into the North Sea. (Depressions lower air pressure and cause the sea level to rise.)

Rising water levels were in turn pushed southwards by winds, now hurricane force. With a record spring tide adding to the surge, an ever-growing wall of water was being forced down the narrowing funnel of the North Sea that separates England from the continental land mass to its narrowest point at the Dover straits.

Along England's East Coast, from early evening, one by one sea defences began to unravel. The first deadly effect of the climatic fury was felt on the Lincolnshire coast at Skegness. Yet the people of Essex were oblivious to the unfolding catastrophe as there was no co-ordinated sea defence warning system.

While people were being drowned in their homes further up the coast, in Harwich cinemagoers patiently queued in the cold and wind for the next performance at the Electric Cinema, yards from the seafront. At Southend a dance was taking place on the pier head with the water rising all around, lapping right up to the boards.

The surge first hit Essex at Harwich. The sea acted as if under military command, determined to smash all resistance before it. Where it couldn't batter down defences it simply rose up and rolled over them. If this was not possible it surrounded the area and attacked from another direction. By midnight Harwich was besieged from three sides with water pouring in and flooding the town.

Further south, the holiday village of Jaywick, just south of Clacton, was picked off in similar fashion. When the water broke through most residents had gone to bed. They were then woken by a tremendous noise and, on opening their front doors to investigate, water crashed in. In the Thames Estuary, by 2.00am, Canvey Island had suffered at least 40 breaches to the sea defences. The Islanders were literally fighting for their lives in the pitch dark.

The surge raced on up the River Thames flooding vast industrial areas. The whole of Tilbury was flooded and even at Westminster the river came perilously close to breaking over the embankments. As the water retreated it left a devastating trail of death and destruction. People were left marooned and traumatised. There were enormous amounts of material damage. Farm animals had died in their thousands and the soil had been ruined. However the fury was not over. On leaving English shores the surge built up again and struck Holland with renewed savagery inflicting widespread damage and claiming over 1800 lives.

Back on Canvey, within days the whole of the Island was evacuated and remained so for months. On Saturday 31st January 1953, Canvey Islanders were proudly saluting the memory of the ultimate sacrifice paid from 5 long years of war. It is difficult to believe that within 5 hours of midnight that figure had been exceeded by the lives lost to the flood on the island alone.

# MAGNOX

*On the banks of the Blackwater, the old Magnox stands,*
*Encased in concrete on the edge of the Dengie lands.*

The credit for inventing the nuclear reactor in 1942 goes to an Italian, Enrico Fermi. The project he was working on resulted in the creation of nuclear weapons which were used to devastating effect to the bring about the end of the Second World War.

After the war, with the destructive power of nuclear fission known, attention was turned again to developing it for peaceful purposes. In Essex, construction of Bradwell nuclear power station began in December 1957. It was the first fully commercial nuclear plant in Britain. One of eleven Magnox nuclear power stations built between 1956 and 1971, Bradwell began generating electricity in 1962. Both the local and national press were enthusiastic about the project. Nuclear power was seen as a solution to the future energy needs of the planet. It was considered to be clean, and although climate change was not an issue then, the nuclear option was believed to be reliable, enduring and above all cheap.

The station was built on the coast of the Dengie peninsula, on the south side of the Blackwater estuary, on the site of the wartime 'Bradwell Bay' airfield. The location was deliberately chosen as it was considered geologically sound with good access by road and by sea. It also had an unlimited source of cooling water from the North Sea.

The term Magnox is short for magnesium non-oxidising, one of the first types of nuclear reactor, but the system was soon obsolete. In theory, at full capacity Bradwell could supply sufficient electricity to power Southend, Colchester and Chelmsford put together but it seldom achieved that. There were continual and growing worries about safety and the problems of dealing satisfactorily with nuclear waste. Fears became acute after the 1979 accident at Three Mile Island in the USA and the 1986 Chernobyl disaster in the former Soviet Union.

In 1999, British Nuclear Fuels announced that Bradwell would cease operation in 2002. It was the first nuclear power station to be closed on a planned basis. Apart from anything else it was no longer economic to operate and electricity generation stopped at Easter. Assembled outside the gates on one side was a small group of people on the verge of tears whilst on the other side was another group applauding and clapping.

It is estimated that 10 years will be needed to decommission and defuel the plant. It is not yet known when the site could be used for other purposes.

# WRITING ON THE WALL

*If you ever come to Walden by the single track,*
*You're advised to place your luggage firmly in the rack,*
*And walk the two odd miles at a steady easy pace,*
*For it will prove the quickest way of getting to the place.*

One hundred years separated the two great eras of railways. The 1860s saw railway building on an unprecedented scale and the 1960s saw a ruthless closure programme. The branch line between Audley End and Saffron Walden was involved in both.

Saffron Walden's branch line opened in 1865. The town council had recommended a link to the London to Cambridge route five years earlier. The necessary capital was raised and parliamentary approval granted. However, even before construction began, there was dissent amongst the directors about extending the line further north to Bartlow. Work on the northern extension proved more challenging due to the hilly terrain as the line approached Bartlow. This stretched finances. Nevertheless the extension was finished 11 months later and by October 1866 the line was in operation along its full length. If nothing else the Victorian railway builders were determined to get their project completed and paid little heed to environmental or archaeological concerns. They were quite content to bulldoze anything that got in the way as was witnessed in the destruction of the Roman barrows at Bartlow. The line was beset with problems from the start. Passenger numbers were less than anticipated and within 10 years the Saffron Walden Railway Company sold out to avoid bankruptcy.

After the Second World War Britain's railways were taken into state ownership. Yet in spite of receiving large amounts from the taxpayer they continued to lose money, passengers and freight. The government's attitude was changing too and railways were no longer seen as the backbone of the economy. Trains were a burden and a financial liability. Motor transport and roads were perceived as the country's future.

In 1961, Dr Richard Beeching was appointed as chairman of British Rail with a task of stemming the losses. His solution was to close 4,000 miles of rail line and 3,000 stations. The plan was put into effect and completed over a 10 year period. The Saffron Walden Branch line was an early casualty in what was known as the Beeching Axe.

Saffron Waldon's last passenger train was the 8.09pm Sunday night service and ran on 7th September 1964. To a certain extent it is surprising the service lasted that long. The 'Writing on the Wall' had been up for sometime, as seen in the edited verse above which was sent by a disgruntled passenger known as *CM* to a local paper fifteen years earlier.

# PIRATE ASHORE
## MY SHIP IS COMING IN

*A vicious snow laden wind hit the ship,*
*The mooring stretched, strained and began to rip.*

Along the Essex Coast at Frinton, on the evening of Wednesday January 19th 1966, it was cold and stormy with snow flurries. Four miles out to sea, just beyond British territorial waters lay the *Mi Amigo,* a converted cargo boat and home to Britain's first 'pirate' radio station, *Radio Caroline.*

Below decks most of the staff, engineers and disc jockeys, including Dave Lee Travis and Tony Blackburn, watched television. They were completely oblivious to the fact that the ship had broken its anchor chain and was being blown towards the shore. Only when a volunteer (Travis) was needed to adjust the television aerial, a regular occurrence that required going on deck, was something judged amiss. Hastily all the DJs, engineers and crew mustered in the lounge with their life jackets ready to hand. Almost immediately there was a great crash and everybody was thrown over as the ship hit the beach broad side on. Fortunately it came to rest between two metal breakwaters. Maybe it was prophetic but the number two on *Radio Caroline's* chart that week was 'My Ship is Coming in' by the Walker Brothers.

*Radio Caroline* had started broadcasting nearly two years earlier when DJ Simon Dee uttered the following words; *"Hello everybody. This is Radio Caroline, broadcasting on 199, your all-day music station".* Today it is difficult to imagine, prior to the arrival of *Radio Caroline,* what little choice listeners had in the way of broadcast music.

What now is classed as pop music was only continuously available from abroad, from stations such *Radio Luxembourg,* which tended to fade out at night, or *Radio Veronica,* a Dutch Radio transmitter based on a ship off the coast of Holland. Back in the sixties Governments discouraged listening to foreign radio stations as they believed the effects could be harmful to the population at large.

It was not on a whim that the first offshore stations were moored off the Essex coast. With their powerful transmitters they were strategically placed to reach audiences in London, East Anglia and the Midlands. In spite of government threats and efforts at discouragement, some millions of people tuned in to these new broadcasters. *Radio London* quickly joined *Caroline,* then *Radio Atlanta* and soon the waters off Essex were crowded with wannabee broadcasters.

The government continued with threats of action against illegal activity on the high seas but did little. It was left to the weather to do the job for them. Which brings us back to the events of Wednesday, January 19th, 1966. A heroic effort by local lifeboat crews ensured the survival of the illustrious DJs and all those aboard.

*Radio Caroline* was back on the air within two months but the days of the 'pirates' were numbered. One of the pirate stations, *Radio City,* was based on Shivering Sands, an old World War II fort in the Thames estuary. A dispute between two rivals about its ownership led to one of the men being shot dead. The government acted swiftly. In 1967 the Marine Offences Act closed most of the Pirate stations.

Six weeks after the new law was enacted the BBC introduced its own national pop music station, *Radio 1,* with none other than Tony Blackburn at the helm.

*For the record Radio Caroline took its name from Caroline Kennedy, daughter of the late U.S. President John F. Kennedy.*

# ESSEX BOYS

*It was 2 to 1 up with seconds to go.*
*Then as tension built came a terrible blow.*
*Germany scored and snatched the match back.*
*The England team was now on the rack.*

## WEMBLEY, 30TH JULY 1966, WORLD CUP FINAL

## RESULT - ENGLAND 4, WEST GERMANY 2.

The result might have been written - Essex 4, Germany 2, since a quartet of 'Essex Boys' played a crucial role in the outcome. The team manager Alf Ramsay came from Dagenham and the Captain, Bobby Moore, who accepted the *Jules Rimet Trophy* for England from the Queen, was a Barking lad. Martin Peters, who scored one of the goals, was from Plaistow, and Geoff Hurst, the hero of the match who scored the other three goals, was considered an honorary Essex Boy since he had spent his best playing years at West Ham.

It was a hot summer's day as the match got under way. After thirteen minutes West Germany took the lead but six minutes later Geoff Hurst, connecting with a Bobby Moore free kick, headed the ball home to level the score. England then took the lead when a deflection from Hurst (again) enabled Martin Peters to smash the ball into goal with his right foot. As the seconds ticked towards the end of normal time, disaster struck when the Germans equalised with virtually the last kick of the game.

The talk by Alf Ramsay at the break between full time and extra time was inspirational in lifting the team's spirits. He refused to let them dwell on tiredness and disappointment. Pointing to the German players he shouted *"look at them, they're finished!"* The manager then eyed his men and spoke calmly saying; *"All right - you let it slip - now start again."* The team's spirits were lifted. Shortly after extra time started Geoff Hurst scored his second goal with a strong shot that bounced on the underside of the crossbar. The German team hotly disputed the goal, the referee was unsure, but the linesman was positive and the goal stood.

There was no doubt about the fourth goal, as in the dying seconds of the game Geoff Hurst picked up yet another pass from Bobby Moore and blasted a shot in from 25 yards.

As Hurst was running down the left wing some spectators had come onto the pitch. This prompted Kenneth Wolstenholme, the BBC commentator, looking at the crowd to excitedly shout into the microphone *"Some of the crowd are on the pitch, they think it's all over,"* then as Hurst's shot hit the roof of the net he completed the sentence with *"It is now"*. These words have become part of footballing legend and are almost as famous as the result itself.

Alf Ramsay, England's most successful manager, was knighted in 1970; He suffered a stroke during the 1998 world cup finals and died in 1999. Bobby Moore, manager of Southend United between 1984 and 1986, died of cancer in 1993.

Geoff Hurst was knighted in 1998; both he and Martin Peters were given the MBE for services to football.

# LET IT ROCK!

*1000s came on foot or by bus, car, train or ferry*
*And it wasn't to Woodstock, Reading or Glastonbury.*
*From Friday to Bank Holiday Monday it was non stop rock*
*With dozens of bands playing around the clock.*

The committee of the Clacton Round Table did not know what they were letting themselves in for when they settled on a proposal before them to replace the 'Annual Donkey Derby' with a different charity fund raiser. Perhaps inadvertently staging the biggest rock concert ever seen in the British Isles wasn't exactly what they had in mind. However that is exactly what happened at Weeley, in Essex, over the August Bank Holiday weekend in 1971.

Advanced purchase tickets for the three-day event were offered at £1.50 and the gate entry price was £2.00. The organisers thought they would do well, with half a dozen local bands, to get an audience of maybe five, maximum ten, thousand. It was an event planned long before the days of the internet, e-mails or mobile phones. Yet, as the Bank Holiday weekend approached, hundreds of people began turning up in the Weeley area and camping out. They came from all over the country, having seen small advertisements in the music press or heard by word of mouth, travelling to Essex by any means possible.

Fortunately the Round Tablers realised in advance that the event was growing exponentially so allowed a professional promoter to look after the bands. No longer were only a rag tag of local musicians billed to appear but alongside them 36 acts were named on the entry ticket alone. These included a pick of the popular musical celebrities of the day such as Rod Steward, Lindisfarne, T. Rex, Edgar Brown, Mungo Jerry, Dave Edmunds and Juicy Lucy.

By the time the first band was due to play at 10.00pm on the Friday an estimated crowd of 100,000 was packed into the site and still more were arriving all the time. At its peak upwards of 150,000 were thought to have attended. The organisers even appealed that no one else turn up but the message didn't get out or, if it did, it wasn't heeded.

It now became a free concert, as it was almost impossible and probably dangerous to try to collect gate money. The great majority who were there spoke of how wonderful it was. There was some trouble between caterers 'the pie men' and the self appointed security guards, the 'Hells Angels', but in general Essex Police reported only a few arrests and localised parking difficulties.

Alas the Clacton Round Table collected little or no money for the good causes and in fact they were lucky not to have been landed with a huge bill for clearing up.

One local farmer collected an unusual souvenir. A double decker bus, used for hospitality and as a changing room for the bands, was left behind by the promoter, who subsequently declined to collect it.

During the festival a public address was made to find 'Wally' who had been separated from his friends. The call of 'Where's Wally'* was taken up by the crowd with its consequent imprint on our language to this day.

* The cry of 'Where's Wally' was claimed to have been first used at every rock concert in England throughout the sixties and seventies but for the benefit of the Essex Hundred we shall give Weeley the credit.

# THE ENTERPRISE HAS LANDED

*It was Stansted's biggest crowd puller to date*
*And perhaps 250,000 visitors passed through the gate?*
*'The Enterprise' was what they'd all come to see,*
*On the fifth of June nineteen-eighty-three.*

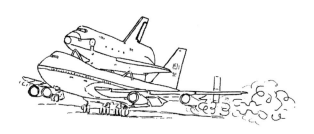

The first 'reusable' manned space vehicle to orbit the earth was the space shuttle *Colombia*. Its maiden flight took place in April 1981. However, before the space shuttle could go into space, it was necessary to prove that it could land back on earth. A specially commissioned prototype space shuttle orbiter was used to test free flight landing procedures. This was called OV101, or more commonly, the *Enterprise*.

Two years later, following the first successful space shuttle flights, the American National Aeronautics and Space Administration (NASA) decided to send the *Enterprise* on a world-wide promotional tour. Stansted was its first port of call in Europe. Originally the proposed name of the 'shuttle' was the *Constitution*. However a massive letter writing campaign by space enthusiasts persuaded the powers that be to change it to that of the craft in the popular science fiction show *Star Trek*.

The space shuttle *Enterprise* landed in Essex, on 5th June 1983, at Stansted Airport. It arrived in style at 15.45, mounted piggyback on top of a modified Boeing 747, although due to the weather it was an hour late. It was a glorious sunny day, the VIPs were all seated and the spectators waited expectantly. It was to be a great photographic occasion to remember and the *Sally B,* the historic B17 World War II bomber, made a fly past before returning to nearby Duxford. Unfortunately two bus loads of press photographers were unable to disembark at the right time to capture the landing moment as they were held back by over enthusiastic security personnel.

The 747 pilot, Fitzhugh Fulton of the United States Airforce, brought his plane to a stop on the concourse to tumultuous applause. The *Enterprise* stayed for two days. Whilst security may have spoilt the press photographer's day they seemed unable to control the numbers of spectators who turned up.

Some estimates put the number of visitors at 250,000 but nobody knows for sure. Whatever the figure, the narrow country lanes around the airport became completely blocked and there was traffic chaos. Stansted airport was in its infancy and parking and the road infrastructure was not what it is today.

One of the best views of the *Enterprise* was from the air and a shrewd operator, based at Southend Airport, offered sightseeing flights using vintage Douglas DC-3 Dakotas.

Although the *Enterprise* only stayed in Essex for two days the visit was a hugely popular success. It is remembered in the corporate address of Stansted Airport, *Enterprise House,* named in honour of the shuttle's visit. On site there is also a meeting room called the *Fulton,* named after the chief pilot *Fitzhugh Fulton.*

The *Enterprise* was built as a test vehicle and was not equipped for, and therefore never experienced, space flight. It is now housed in a museum just outside Washington DC in the USA. The original fully fledged space shuttle *Colombia,* the first shuttle to fly in space, disintegrated during re-entry on its 28th mission, on 1 February 2003. All seven crew members aboard perished.

The 5th June 2008 marked the 25th Anniversary of the shuttle's visit to Essex. To mark the occasion Derek Winter of BBA Stansted organised a special reunion celebration in Enterprise House including the making of an 'Enterprise' cake. 2008 also marked the 50th anniversary of NASA.

# LAMBS TO THE SLAUGHTER

*1,000 people faced the driver on that first night*
*Having been out since dawn to exert their right.*

It all began on 16th January 1995. It 'ended' on Monday 30th October. For nine months the small Essex town of Brightlingsea had been traumatised by the events that took place. One man had died, 598 people had been arrested and 1200 complaints had been made against the police. Thousands of pounds worth of damage had been inflicted on the port area and the cost of policing during all this was estimated at five million pounds. Many protesters had lost their jobs and businesses had been ruined. It would take a long time for all the wrongs to be put right and longer for the psychological scars to be healed.

At the centre of the conflict that produced all this fury was the export of live animals to the continent, especially lambs and veal calves. The trade had been going on for years but with increasing difficulty for exporters. A growing, and increasingly militant, animal rights movement was completely opposed to it and the harsh conditions in which the animals were transported. It was the latter, the unacceptable and inhumane way the animals were transported, that drew an even wider public support to the protest.

Many ports such as Shoreham, Plymouth, Dover and Kings Lynn had already faced the fury of demonstrators and ceased shipments.

As a result Brightlingsea, almost by default, became the chosen place for a showdown. A determined exporter and a cooperative port owner had joined forces. After all the Government, in the shape of DEFRA* had ruled that, notwithstanding that the welfare of animals was paramount, this was a lawful trade. During the course of 10 months 174 convoys carrying 150,000 sheep and 60,000 veal calves passed through Brightlingsea. The animals were then shipped to Belgium on the MV Caroline. (There was no connection with the pirate radio station of the same name.)

Protesters, often numbered in their thousands, made determined efforts to halt the shipments. At times the police invoked the public order act and several injunctions were taken out against leading protesters. On occasions the demonstration turned violent when tempers were lost. The ranks of the protesters, largely peaceful but vociferous, were swollen at times by agitators whose sole purpose was to cause trouble and violence. In their turn the police were frequently accused of heavy handedness.

There appeared to be no winners except perhaps just one. A sheep was 'kidnapped' from the port by protesters and christened 'Lucky the Lamb'. Lucky never went to Belgium and presumably survived to a ripe old age.

Then, without warning, on Monday 30th October 1995 shipments ceased. Protesters were waiting as usual, but no lorries came. The principal exporter decided it was uneconomical to continue. There were no further shipments and Brightlingsea stopped being a focal point of protest.

After a stiff legal fight, trade resumed at Dover. Nearly one million live animals were exported annually from the UK until 2001. When foot and mouth disease broke out in February that year the trade in live animal export ceased. Restrictions were lifted in July 2002. Another foot and mouth outbreak happened in the summer of 2007. Live animal exports (2008) are estimated at approximately 60,000 per annum, over 90% down on the pre 2001 figure.

*DEFRA: Department for Environment, Food and Rural Affairs*

**Lucky the Lamb**
**The One That Got Away**

# WINDMILLS ON MY MIND

*From Dagenham's industrial heartland they creep,*
*Across Essex, to the sea. They never sleep,*
*They buzz and whirr, speaking to their own kind*
*But not to me, or the windmills on my mind.*

Windmills have been around in Essex for more than 600 years. Generally used for pumping water or grinding flour, they reached their greatest numbers in the 1830s. Within 30 years however many mills were struggling to survive. Wind power was competing with new, more reliable power sources which were becoming available - coal-fired steam engines, oil-burning engines, followed by electricity from the national grid. The agricultural depressions of the late nineteenth century and industrialisation tipped the scales against windmill operators and hundreds closed as a consequence. Many were demolished; others were just abandoned and left derelict and by 1950 nearly all had ceased to be used commercially. Many of the windmills we see today owe their existence to their status as heritage attractions maintained by dedicated bands of volunteers.

Traditional windmills were basically of three types. First were the *Post* mills, so named because of the large upright post on which the mill's main structure balanced. This allowed the whole mill to rotate according to the wind direction. Bocking Mill near Braintree, built in 1721, is a good example.

The next development was the *Smock* mill. The *Smock* mill that remains in Upminster was built in 1803 by local farmer, James Noake. The name is attributed to their resemblance to the smock, or dress-like agricultural costume, worn by most farm labourers of the day. The wooden body of this type of mill no longer rotated, only the cap holding the sails turned to follow the wind.

Lastly came, *Tower* mills. They were a refinement of the *Smock* mill. The wooden body was replaced with a fixed brick or stone built tower. A lovingly restored *Tower* mill, originally put up in 1816, may be seen standing in the village of Stock.

The sophisticated manufacturing and technology that had caused the demise of the windmill was however subject to a new threat. It had become totally reliant upon OIL! In the 1970s Arab – Israeli wars sent shock waves throughout England and the world. The cost of oil surged. Concern, even alarm, was expressed over the security of supply. There were also growing worries over the effect on the planet's environment of burning fossil fuels which resulted in a determined search for alternative energy sources. The wheel had turned full circle and windmills, in the form of wind turbines, were looked to as a possible solution.

Essex is in the vanguard of development. The two wind turbines erected by Ford Motor Company at Dagenham, in April 2004, have shown what can be achieved. Nearly the same height as The London Eye, each stands 120 metres tall.

The design principle used is the same as the old *Smock* mill where the metal tower is fixed. The cap that houses the generator and carries the turbine blades rotates according to wind direction. Enough power is generated from these two turbines to meet the energy needs of Ford's new state of the art Diesel Assembly Hall. To achieve this 1800-kilowatt power requirement wind speed must reach 13 miles per hour. If this speed is not achieved then electricity is drawn from the national grid. Conversely, if there is surplus electricity created this is then fed into the national grid.

A third turbine is being planned on the Dagenham site, which will enable the power needs of the whole estate to be met. So successful has the scheme been that the 2012 Olympics Delivery Authority has assessed the Ford site and is considering building a comparable scheme in the River Lea valley.

Further east in the county another project has fared less well. Close to Bradwell-on-Sea, construction of 26 wind turbines was envisaged, each one similar in height to those at Dagenham, but following fierce local opposition the numbers were reduced to ten. A radio documentary on the subject compared the scale of protest raised as being on a par with that seen during the operation of Bradwell's Magnox nuclear power station.

Other wind farm schemes are equally beset by problems. Proposals to build five turbines at Earls Hall Farm near Clacton were rejected by Tendering District Council in June 2008. Further east again, offshore from Clacton and stretching south into the Thames Estuary plans for - 'The London Array' are well advanced. If the 271 turbines envisaged are built, they will occupy an area of sea greater than the land covered by Southend-on-Sea, Rochford, Castle Point and Basildon councils combined. The power output is forecast to be 10 times greater than the old Bradwell nuclear power station. However one of the projects major backers pulled out early in 2008.

If the wheel really has turned full circle for wind power, then windmills may well be here for another 600 years or so. Whether they will be commercially viable then or just heritage landmarks is another matter.

# THE ESSEX COAT OF ARMS

### The Seax

Throughout Essex the county coat of arms appears on village and town signs, school name boards, fire engines, police helmets and county council vehicles. It is also prominently displayed when entering the county by main roads.

The coat of arms consists of three seaxes placed one above the other. The seax is a curved sword or knife with a hilt, its handle terminating in a pommel or knob. There is a semi circular notch on the back of each blade and they are believed to have evolved from Saxon short swords which were originally 21 – 46 cms long and about 5 cms deep. The official coat of arms colours are:-

> *Gules, three Seaxes fessewise in pale Argen, pomels*
> *[knobs] and hilts [handles] or, pointed to the*
> *sinister and cutting edges upwards.*

In plain English this is; silver for the seax with the cutting edge upwards and the pommel pointing to the left, shown on a red shield.

There is an element of mystery as to why Essex adopted the seax. In the *Anglo Saxon Chronicles* Essex is called *Eastseaxe*. Study by historians and heraldic experts suggest something similar to the Essex coat of arms was used in the East Saxon kingdom over 1000 years ago. However the Saxons were decisively defeated by King Knut's (Canute) Danish Vikings at the Battle of Ashingdon in 1016. King Canute became the undisputed King of England and the Saxon rulers fled west or went into exile. Although the Saxons returned following the death of King Canute they were again crushed by the Normans in the Battle of Hastings in 1066.

The Essex coat of arms appeared in print more or less as it is today, but with a Saxon crown above it, in John Speed's 1623 book *'Historie of Great Britaine'*. It would seem safe to assume that it was in use long before that.

With the growth of printing more and more Essex towns, villages and organisations adopted the emblem. Surprisingly it was not until 1932 that the College of Arms officially granted Essex its current coat of arms.

# THE ESSEX WAY

*From Epping through Ongar and Fyfield go*
*Past Willingale's two churches - Spain and Doe.*
*Through Good Easter, past Pleshey's old Motte and Bailey*
*To Great Waltham, Terling and up to White Notley.*
*Now Cressing's Barns where Knights Templar once stayed,*
*A short walk to Coggeshall and the journey's half made.*
*By way of Great Tey, West Bergholt and Boxted*
*Arrive at Dedham where Constable once painted.*
*After Mistley, Manningtree, Ramsey and Little Oakley*
*Reach Harwich the end of this eighty-one mile journey.*

The Essex Way meanders northwesterly across the county starting at London's Central Line tube station at Epping and continuing to the port of Harwich. It is a long distance footpath that, following ancient rights of way, links many of the places and events mentioned in previous chapters.

At Epping the outlaw Dick Turpin laid low in the Forest. If David Livingstone had followed the Essex Way he may have arrived back in Ongar in time for dinner. A few miles further along Willingale's two churches stand side by side on the same plot of land, but no squabbling sisters are to be seen. The footpath passes through Pleshey, mentioned in William Shakespeare's Richard II. Leaving Pleshey, the route traverses lands and manors formerly owned by the dynastic de Vere family and then by Essex bad boy Richard Riche. At Cressing the original granary barns still stand that served as storehouses for the Knights Templars. Turning east the path follows the River Blackwater leaving it to arrive at Coggeshall, the halfway point of the journey. Fortunately the gang that once terrorised the area, much like Dick Turpin did in Epping a hundred years before, has long gone.

Leaving Coggeshall, the Essex Way runs close to Boxted Hall where Edward III once spent the night on a secret assignation much to the chagrin of the citizens of Colchester. In 1648, during the English Civil War, fleeing Royalists, hotly pursued by Parliamentary forces, followed a route almost identical to the Essex Way travelling from London to Colchester.

From Boxted the way enters Constable Country passing right by John Constable's old school in Dedham. A few miles further on, nestling the banks of the River Stour, the old Manningtree haunts of the Witch Finder General, Matthew Hopkins reveal themselves. Just outside the town, legions of swans boldly strut up and down. Their ancestors would have much to tell if questioned. Richard Rigby's great folly, the twin towers at Mistley, loom into view. Following the banks of the Stour to Harwich, on the North Sea coast, the 81 miles of the Essex Way ends at the high lighthouse. The port was once the Parliamentary seat of Samuel Pepys and the birthplace of exploring sea captains Christopher Jones and Christopher Newport, the men who steered colonists to unknown fates in the New World.

Stunning scenery, mystery, intrigue, adventure and years of history - the Essex Way has them all.

## LOCATIONS AND CONTACT ADDRESSES
(By subject)

**Armageddon**
Kelvedon Hatch Secret Nuclear Bunker
Kelvedon Hall Lane
Great Myles Ongar Road
Kelvedon Hatch CM14 5TZ
Tel: 01277 364 883
*www.japar.demon.co.uk*

**Bertram the Clown**
Clacton Pier
Tel: 01255 421115

**Billericay Pioneers**
Cater Museum
74 High Street
Billericay Essex
CM12 9BS
Tel: 01277 622023
*E-mail: cater-museum@supanet.com*
*www.catermuseum.co.uk*

**Boudica and Under Seige**
Colchester Castle Museum, Castle Park
Colchester CO1 1YG
Tel: 01206 282939
*www.colchestermuseums.org.uk*
Tourist Information Centre Colchester
Tel: 01206 282290
e-mail: vic@colchester.gov.uk

**Chapel on the Wall**
The Chapel of St Peter-on-the-Wall
Bradwell-on-Sea, Essex
Othona Community Enquiries
Tel: 0621 776564

**Coalhouse Fort and It's Not Cricket**
Coalhouse Fort, Princess Margaret Road
East Tilbury Village, Tilbury RM11 2AS
Tel: 01375 844203
*www.coalhousefort.co.uk*

**Dear Diary**
Audley End House and Gardens
Saffron Walden CB11 4JF
Tel: 01799 522399
*www.english-heritage.org.uk*

**Dissolution**
Leez Priory, Hartford End
Great Leighs, Chelmsford CM3 1JP
Tel: 01245 362 555
*www.brideshead.co.uk/leez*

**Dunmow Flitch and Doctor's Pond**
Great Dunmow Museum, Mill Lane
Dunmow, Essex, CM6 1BG
Tel: 01371 878979
*www.greatdunmowmuseum.org.uk*
*www.dunmowflitchtrials.co.uk*
Dunmow Community Information Office
Council Offices, Great Dunmow
Tel: 01799 510490

**The Duke of Boulogne**
Mountfitchet Castle
Stansted Mountfitchet
Essex CM24 8SP
Tel: 01279 813237
*www.mountfitchetcastle.com*

**Dutch Cottage Museum**
Canvey Road, Canvey Island
Tel: 01268 794005

**Elected by 32**
Harwich Guildhall, Church Street, Harwich
Tel: 01255 503429

**Family Courtauld**
Braintree District Museum
Manor St, Braintree, CM7 3HT
Tel: 01376 325266
*www.enjoybraintreedistrict.co.uk/museum*

**Fairlop Frigate**
Valence House Museum
Becontree Avenue
Dagenham
RM8 3HT
Tel: 020 8270 6865

**Grave Diggers**
Chelmsford Cathedral
New Street Chelmsford CM1 1TY
Tel: 01245 294480
*www.chelmsfordcathedral.org.uk*

**Harbingers at Harlow**
Museum of Harlow
Muskham Road, (off First Avenue)
Harlow, Essex CM20 2LF
Tel: 01279 454959
*www.harlow.gov.uk*

**John Constable's Schooldays**
Constable Country
Bridge Cottage, Flatford, Dedham C07 60L
Tel: 01206 298260
*www.nationaltrust.org.uk/flatford*

**Joscelyne's Beach**
Adjacent to Chalkwell railway station
Southend-on-Sea
(See bibliography – Joscelyne, Arthur.)

**Just Mad about Saffron**
Saffron Walden Museum, Museum Street
Saffron Walden, Essex CB10 1JL
Tel: 01799 510333/4
Uttlesford Tourist and Community Information Centre
1 Market Place, Saffron Walden, Essex CB10 1HR
Tel: 01799 510444
*www.uttlesford.gov.uk*

**Layer Marney Tower**
Maldon Road, (Signposted from B1022)
Layer Marney, Colchester CO5 9US
Tel: 01206 330784
*www.layermarneytower.co.uk*

**Little Ships to Dunkirk**
The Endeavour Trust
Keith Threadgold, Secretary
44 Lansdowne Avenue
Leigh-on-Sea SS9 1LL
Tel: 01702 713 325

**Longer than a Mile**
Southend Pier Museum
Southend Pier, Western Esplanade
Southend-on-Sea SS1 1EE
Tel: 01702 611214
*www.southendpiermuseum.co.uk*

**Magna Carta (de Vere's) and Dog of War**
Hedingham Castle
Castle Hedingham, Essex. CO9 3DJ
Tel: 01787 460261
*www.hedinghamcastle.co.uk*

**Magnox**
Bradwell Nuclear Power Station
Bradwell-on-Sea
Southminster CM0 7HP
Tel: 01621 776331
*www.britishnucleargroup.com*

**Not a lot of people know that.**
Tourist Information Centre Waltham Abbey
Highbridge Street, Waltham Abbey, EN9 1DG
Tel: 01992 652295
and also the Abbey
The Parish Office, 5a Greenyard
Waltham Abbey, Essex, EN9 1RD
Tel: 01992 767897
*www.walthamabbeychurch.co.uk*

**Onward Christian Soldiers**
St Edmunds Church, East Mersey
Church Lane, Mersey Essex

**Pirate Ashore**
Radio Caroline
The Maidstone Studios, Vinters Park
Maidstone, Kent ME14 5NZ
Tel: 01622 684400
*www.radiocaroline.co.uk*

**Plotlanders**
Langdon Visitor's Centre
Third Avenue, Lower Dunton Road
Basildon SS16 6EB
Tel: 01268 419103
*www.ukattraction.com/east-of-england/langdon-visitors-centre*

**Radio 2MT**
Chelmsford Visitor Information Centre
Chelmsford Rail Station
Duke Street, Chelmsford CM1 1HT
Tel: 01245 283400
*www.marconicalling.com*

**Sad Days at High Beech**
Epping Forest Visitors Centre
Nursery Road, High Beach, Epping
Tel: 0208 8508 0028
*www.cityoflondon.gov.uk*

**Salvation Army Colony**
Salvation Army, Hadleigh Farm
Castle Lane, Benfleet SS7 2AP
Tel: 01702 558550
*www.hadleighfarm.co.uk*

**Sea Witch and Leigh Fishy Tales**
Leigh Heritage Centre
13a High Street
Leigh-On-Sea SS9 2EN
Tel: 01702 470834
*http://www.leighsociety.co.uk/leighheritagecentre.htm*

**Thames Barge**
Topsail Charters
Cooks Barge Yard
The Hythe, Maldon CM9 5HN
Tel: 01621 857567

**Thaxted**
Thaxted Information Centre
7 Town Street, Thaxted CM6 2PJ
Tel: 01371 831641
*www.thaxted.co.uk*

**Three Days that shook the Kingdom**
Brentwood Tourist Information Centre
44 High St, Brentwood CM14 4AJ
Tel: 01277 200300

**Three Mills at Battlesbridge**
Battlesbridge Antiques Centre
Hawk Hill, Battlesbridge SS11 7RE
Tel: 01268 575000 / 764197
*www.battlesbridge.com*

**Tiptree Jam**
Wilkin & Sons Limited
Tiptree CO5 0RF
Tel: 01621-814524 (Visitor centre)
*www.tiptree.com*

**Walton Tower**
Walton on the Naze
Tel: 07966776417
The Naze Protection Society
Tel: 01255 676868
*www.ukattraction.com/east-of-england/naze-tower*

**'Waterway to Chelmsford'**
Chelmer Canal Trust
Windmill Pasture, Little Waltham Road
Chelmsford, Essex CM1 7TG
*www.chelmercanaltrust.co.uk*

**William Byrd**
Stondon Place, Stondon Massey
Also Ingatestone Hall
Ingatestone CM4 9NR
Tel: 01277 353010

**William Morris**
William Morris Gallery
Lloyd Park, Forest Road
London E17 4PP
Tel: 020 8527 3782
*www.walthamforest.gov.uk/wmg/*

## FOR MORE GENERAL RESEARCH

**Essex County Council Libraries**
PO Box 882, Market Road
Chelmsford CM1 1LH
Telephone: 01245 492758
*www.essexcc.gov.uk/libraries*

**Essex Records Office**
Wharf Road
Chelmsford CM2 6YT
Tel: 01245 244644
*www.essexcc.gov.uk/ero*

**Southend on Sea Libraries**
Southend Central Library
Victoria Avenue
Southend SS2 6EX
Tel. 01702 534100
*www.southend.gov.uk*

**Thurrock Libraries**
Thameside Complex, Orsett Road
Grays RM17 5DX
*www.thurrock.gov.uk/libraries*

Whilst every care has been taken to ensure the accuracy of the above information the editors are unable to accept responsibility for its content which has been supplied in good faith.

## ABOUT THE AUTHORS

### ANDREW SUMMERS
*Born within the sound of Bow Bells, Andrew has lived for the last 18 years in Hadleigh and been married to Glenis for 41 years. Andrew has bought books, sold books, printed books and now decided to write and publish books too! He was one of the few people to turn down a job from Alan Sugar.*

### JOHN DEBENHAM
*Born in Romford John has always lived in Essex. On retirement from engineering he took a BA History degree followed by an MA in Intellectual History, studying 'Civilisation and Barbarism'. A member of Southend Poetry Society and Rocheway writing group he enjoys historical research, and writes poetry and short stories with longer works in 'perpetual progress'.*

### AND THE ARTIST: ELIZABETH SUMMERS
*Elizabeth lives in Suffolk and is a member of the Sudbourne Park Printmakers Group. She has illustrated several books and is an accomplished printmaker and painter in oils. Her work is regularly exhibited locally and was featured prominently at Aldeburgh's Peter Pears Gallery Easter showing as well as the recent Art Expo in Antwerp in Belgium.*


## AND THE CONTRIBUTING POETS

*SHIRLEY BAKER - (Dunmow Flitch, Tiptree Jam, Harbingers at Harlow, Dutch Cottage, Walton Tower, Missing Person from Harlow and The Little Ships of Leigh) Shirley lives in Leigh-on-Sea, Essex and has been writing for many years. She is a member of the Southend Poetry Group and has published poems on a wide variety of subjects.*

*JOHN F BARR - (Happy Harry) Born in Essex John worked as a Chartered Surveyor until retiring in 2005. He has had several poems published in the Southend Poetry Group's anthologies.*

*CHRISTINE BILLINGTON - (Boadica's Revenge and William Morris) Writing since a teenager Christine has had several collections of poetry published by K.T. Publications and many pieces taken by small press publishers.*

*CLARE HARVEY - (Joscelyne's Beach Chalkwell) Born in Wiltshire, but of an old Leigh bloodline, since retirement, in 2001, Clare concentrates on 5 grandchildren, poetry, photography, painting, gardening, swimming and long term partner - Mervyn!*

*MERVYN LINFORD* - *(Three Mills at Battlesbridge and Mulberry)* Mervyn has been writing for over thirty years. He has had work published in many magazines, periodicals and anthologies and has been broadcast on both local and national radio. He has had seven collections of poetry published and four works of prose. He runs the 'Littoral Press' and is Poetry Editor for 'Pentangle' magazine.

*KATIE MALLETT* - *(Coalhouse Fort)* Katie has written poems and articles since the 1980s. Her work has appeared in Essex magazines and newspapers, and various anthologies, including a series of books edited by E.O. Parrott published by Penguin/Viking.

*ADRIAN GREEN* - *(Sweyn's Castle)* Adrian Green lives overlooking the sea at Southend. He holds degrees in psychology and general arts as well as a Post Graduate Diploma in Humanities. He is a former editor of SOL magazine, and reviews editor of Littoral Press. He has published 2 pamphlet collections – 'Beachgame' and 'The Watchers'. His most recent book 'Chorus and Coda' was published in 2007.

*MARGARET RICE* - *(Witnesses in White)* Margaret, who died in 2006, had a love of language and literature throughout her life. A move to Essex in 2003 focused her writing and particularly poetry allowing her to produce some of her most observant and poignant work.

# SELECTED BIBLIOGRAPHY

Addison, William, *Essex Worthies : a biographical companion to the County,* Phillimore, 1973.

Adkin, Mark, *The Trafalgar Companion,* Aurum Press Ltd, 2005.

Anderson, Verily, *The de Veres of Castle Hedingham,* Terence Dalton, 1993.

Backscheider, Paula, R., *Daniel Defoe,* John Hopkins University, 1989.

Basildon Branch Libraries, *Billericay and the New World: a summary,* Essex County Library, 1970.

Bailey, Anthony, *John Constable, a Kingdom of His Own,* Chatto & Windus, 2006.

Benham, Hervey, *Some Essex Water Mills,* Essex County Newspapers Ltd, 1976.

Benham, Hervey, *The Smuggler's Century: The Story of Smuggling on the Essex Coast 1750 – 1830,* Essex Record Office Publications, 1986.

Bingley, Randal, *Fobbing, Life and Landscape,* Thurrock Museum, 1997.

Bingley, Randal, *Panorama* Thurrock Local History Society, various 1985 - 2007.

Booth William General, *In Darkest England,* Charles Knight and Co. Ltd., 1970.

Brewer, John, *Sentimental Murder,* Harper Perennial, 2005.

Bush, Reg, *Sandon A Village History,* Reg Bush, 1999.

Caffrey, Kate, *The Mayflower,* Andre Deutsch, 1975.

Carney, Terry, *Thurrock in the Thirties,* Thurrock Museum Publications, 2005.

Carpenter R.J., *Christopher Martin Great Burstead and The Mayflower,* Barnstable Books, 1982.

Carter, Douglas, *Short History of Boxted,* 1996.

Carter, M.H., *The Fort of Othona and the Chapel of St Peter-on-the-Wal,.* Provost and Chapter of Chelmsford, 1966.

Chelmsford Museum Service, *Guglielmo Marconi, 1874-1937 : The Father of Wireless.* Chelmsford Museum Service, 1987.

Chisenhale-Marsh, T.C.(Trans.), *Domesday Book relating to Essex.* W.D. Burrell, 1864.

Clark, Dr. Michael, *Rochford Hall : the history of a Tudor house and biographies of its owners,* Alan Sutton, 1990.

Colthorpe, M and Bateman, *L.H. Queen Elizabeth I and Harlow.* Harlow Development Corporation, 1997.

Coote, Stephen, *Samuel Pepys a Life,* Sceptre Hodder & Stoughton, 2001.

Currie, I. Davidson, M. Ogley, R. *The Essex Weather Book,* Froglets, 1992.

Davis, G. R. C., *Magna Carta,* British Museum, 1965.

Dudley, Donald.R, *The Rebellion of Boudicca,* Routledge and Kegan Paul, 1962.

Dury, John, *A History of Felsted,* John Dury, 1999.

Egerton, Judy, *Turner The Fighting Temeraire,* National Gallery Publications, 1995.

Embleton, Paul, *Around Stansted Mountfitchet,* Tempus Publishing, 1999.

Federation of Essex Womens Institutes (Compiled by), *Essex Village Book,* Countryside, 2001.

Garwood, Ivan, *Mistley in the days of the Rigbys,* Lucas Books, 2003.

Gould, Rev. Sabine Baring-Gould, *Mehalah,* Boydell, 1983.

Green, Georgina, *The Story of Hainault Forest,* London Borough of Redbridge Library Services, 2001.

Grieve, Hilda, *The Sleepers and the Shadows, Volumes I and II,* Essex Records Office, 1988 and 1994.

Grun, Bernard, *The Timetables of History,* Simon and Schuster, 1982.

Hallman, Robert, *South Benfleet a History,* Phillimore, 2005.

Hartcup, Guy, *Code Name Mulberry,* David and Charles, 1977.

Humphries, Ralph, C. *Radio Caroline: the pirate years.* Oakwood, 2003.

Jacobs, Norman, *Clacton on Sea: a Pictorial History,* Phillimore, 1993.

Jarvis, Stan, *Smuggling in East Anglia 1700 – 1840,* Countryside Books, 1987.

Jones, Phil, *The Siege of Colchester 1648,* Tempus Publishing Ltd, 2003.

Joscelyne, Arthur, *Joscelyne's beach : a memoir of Leigh-on-Sea,* Desert Island Books, 2004.

Joscelyne, Arthur, *Joscelyne's tales of old Leigh and Chalkwel,* Desert Island, 2005.

Killick, Jennifer, *Sea Fencibles 1805,* Jennifer Killick, 2001.

Knights, E. Spurgeon, *William Byrd and Stondon Massey : a great musician and his life in Essex,* Essex Review, 1934.

Lake, Hazel, *The Arkwrights and Harlow,* (the author)1996.

Latham, R. and Matthews,W, Eds. *The Diary of Samuel Pepys,* Bell & Hyman, 1983.

Lemmon, David & Marshall, Mike, *Essex County Cricket Club,* Kingswood Press, 1987.

Lewis, Jim, *London's Lea Valley : Britain's best kept secret,* Phillimore, 1999.

Lister, Keith, *Half My Life, The Story of Sabine Baring-Gould and Grace,* Charnwood Publications, 2002.

Lockwood, Martin, *The Coggeshall Gang,* Essex Police Museum, 1995.

MacCamley, N. J, *Cold War Secret Nuclear Bunkers,* Leo Cooper, 2002.

Male, Dr D A. and Kemp-Luck, Mrs A. (Compiled by), *From Serf to Citizen,* Harwich Town Council, 2004.

Martin, Frank, *Rogues River,* Ian Hendry, 1983.

Martin, John, *Beyond Belief. The Real Life of Daniel Defoe,* Accent Press Ltd, 2006.

Marriage, John, *Barging into Chelmsford : the story of the Chelmer and Blackwater navigation,* Ian Hendry, 1997.

Marsden, Barry M, *The Early Barrow Diggers,* Tempus, 1999.

Morgan, Glyn, *Essex Witches : the witches, enchantments, charms and sorcerers of Essex.* Spurbooks, 1973.

Morgan, Glyn, *Secret Essex,* Ian Hendry, 1994.

Morris, Richard, *The Harveys of Rolls Park Chigwell Essex,* Loughton and District Historical Society, 2005.

National Trust Local Committee, *Rayleigh Mount,* 1965.

Neale, Kenneth, *Essex 'full of profitable thinges',* Leopard's Head Press, 1996.

O'Leary, J.G, *The Book of Dagenham,* Borough of Dagenham, 1964.

Parkhill, Gordon and Cook, Graham, *Hadleigh Salvation Army Farm, A Vision Reborn,* Salvation Army Shield Books, 2008.

Pitt-Stanley, Sheila, *Legends of Leigh,* Pitt-Stanley, 1989.

Powles, John, *Iron in the Blood,* Tony Brown, 2005.

Pratt, Barbara, *The Loppers of Loughton,* Barbara Pratt Publications, 1981.

Price, Harry, *The Most Haunted House in England : ten years' investigation of Borley Rectory,* Chivers Press, 1975.

Rumble, Alexander, Editor, *Doomsday Book Essex,* Phillimore, 1983.

Scott, E.V, *The Best of Essex Countryside* County Guide Publications, 1976.

Scott, Winifred N, *Coryton. History of a Village,* Mobil, 1981.

Sharpe, James, *Dick Turpin - The Myth of the English Highwayman,* Profile Books, 2005.

Shepherd, E.W, *The Story of Southend Pier - and its associations,* Egon, 1979.

Sipple, Mavis, *Rochford A History,* Phillimore, 2004.

Smith, Graham, *Smuggling in Essex,* Countryside Books, 2005.

Smith, Michael. *I am just going outside: Captain Oates - Antarctic tragedy,* Spellmount, 2002.

Smith, Victor T.C, *Coalhouse Fort,* Essex County Council, 1985.

Tomalin, Claire, *Samuel Pepys The Unequalled Self,* Viking Penguin, 2002.

Vingoe, Lesley, *Hockley, Hullbridge and Hawkwell Past,* Phillimore, 1999.

Webber, Ronald, *Peasants Revolt,* Terrance Dalton, 1980.

Williams, Judith, *Leigh-on-Sea: A History,* Phillimore, 2002.

Wood, Robert, *The Widow of Borley,* Duckworth, 1992.

Yearsley, Ian, *Essex Events : death, disaster, war and weather,* Phillimore, 1999.

Yearsley, Ian, *Hadleigh Past.* Phillimore, 1998.

Yearsley, Ian, *Rayleigh a History,* Phillimore, 2005.

Yearsley Ian, *History of Southend,* Phillimore, 2001.

## Pamphlets

Steer, F.W., *The Coat of Arms of the County of Essex,* ERO Pamphlet No 2 Essex Records Office, 1949

## Magazines & Newspapers.

"The Public Hell of Happy Harry" by Leslie Salisbury in *Evening Echo, November 30th, 1972.*

Full account of the calamitous earthquake in East Essex on Tuesday morning, April 22nd 1884: reprinted from *The Essex Telegraph.* Frederic Wright, 1884.

# NOTES